Jennifer Heather

About the Author

Jennifer Heather is a seamstress and writer located on the south coast of England. She crafts bewitching clothing in her online store Obsidian Siren, and has channelled her passion for all things metaphysical and occult into writing. What began as a series of mini e-books has now been curated into a compendium of work that encapsulates her affinity to Greek mythology. A graduate from Bournemouth University where she studied psychology, the work of Carl Jung initiated a keen interest in the subconscious mind, which in turn opened the door to other esoteric topics.

Contents

Introduction

They say knowledge is power, so is it any wonder that divination, the art of obtaining knowledge of the future or insights into unknowable information through supernatural methods, has been a part of human culture since ancient times. Driven by an unquenchable thirst for knowledge, mankind has devised a myriad of methods to divine the unknown, offering a tantalizing glimpse into what lies ahead. From Tarot cards to scrying, the object is usually to gain insight, make decisions, understand the motivations of others, or obtain clarity on past events. Divination offers us more than a glimpse into a possible future though; it also provides us with a glimpse into our self. As a tool of personal development, performing a reading can help the individual to explore their psyche by offering up a canvas onto which we may project our feelings. When abstract symbols are used in place of words, it helps us bypass the logical, analytical part of the mind and allows us to connect with the heart of what troubles us. There is something viscerally pleasing too, about casting a handful of small objects and observing how they land; the fall of the stones is influenced by the hand of fate.

Practices such as the Tarot require the reader to study the deck carefully so that they may understand the complexity and nuance of the symbology woven throughout the 78 cards. It can take years to become comfortable with performing a Tarot reading, whereas other folk methods of divination are more intuition based. Lithomancy, for example, is the art of divination through stone throwing. Stones, crystals, or other small objects are tossed onto the ground or grid so the pattern they create can be interpreted. Lewis (1999) states 'The stones are tossed and a prophecy is drawn from the arrangement in which the stones land'. We can see how Lithomancy overlaps with rune reading, both relying on the casting of lots. Whilst the Elder Futhark runes may be counted amongst the most well known runic methods, the ancient Greeks employed a form of dice divination that could be viewed as a precursor to rune reading. This dice based divination (astragalomancy) known known as "astragalizein," refers to the use of astragali, or knuckle bones, as the casting objects. These knuckle bones were typically derived from the ankle bones of sheep or goats and were marked with different symbols or numbers. It would be wonderful to implement this ancient practice, but unfortunately the specific details have not been preserved. However, witches are nothing if not resourceful, creating new systems of divining that utilize the symbols that exist within the collective.

When I first discovered the Witches' runes I was immediately enchanted by their beauty; the elegant yet simple glyphs of these runes resonated with me at once. A relatively new system of divination on the grand scheme, created by witches for witches. My first set came with a leaflet that summarized each of the thirteen runes in a short sentence, meaning I began my runic practice with very little to go on. This didn't impede my experience with the runes though as I felt that the symbols were straightforward enough to allow my intuition to guide my readings. Eventually though, I wanted a little more knowledge so that I could deepen my connection to the symbology of the runes. However, when reading one of the few books that had been published about the Witches' runes, I found that the meanings didn't quite line up with how I had come to know them. The most recent book on the subject was written in 1998 by author Susan Sheppard, and the meanings reflected her own eclectic approach to divination. It is my intention now to offer an evolutionary update to the Witches' runes. A set of meanings that reflects current attitudes and interpretations of the world. The concept of assigning an astrological zodiac sign to the runes has been upheld, but some of the associations have been switched. Notably, the Harvest rune now corresponds with the zodiac sign of Virgo rather than Sagittarius. These changes are discussed in more detail in the relevant section for each of the rune symbols. Greek myths have been woven in with the explanations of each rune as a way to communicate the archetypal energy that the symbols hold. Ancient Greece has been hugely influential on Western culture, therefore the stories and myths are known to us even if we don't realise it. Our media is dominated by subtle references and retellings of these enduring stories that feel as familiar as an old friend. There is no requirement for you to believe in deities of any form when using the Witches' runes, their inclusion is a mechanism that might help you to grasp the key symbology of the symbols, making it easier for you to perform readings.

As always, this book is for everyone. Take what resonates and leave what doesn't.

History of Runes

Before we explore the Witches' runes, let's examine what runes are. It is possible that the word 'rune' may conjure up images of the Norse rune symbols; the set of 24 characters made from vertical, horizontal and diagonal lines that forms the alphabet of old Germanic languages. The simplistic, angular design of the runes is thought to have been a deliberate style choice to make them easy to carve onto wood or stone. This made runic use accessible to everyone, as natural materials such as wood and stone are freely available (Saille, 2009). Today, the only surviving examples we have of runic writings are those carved into stone, thanks to its durable nature.

There are numerous runic alphabets that have been created throughout the course of human existence; runes are essentially symbols that communicate information. The word 'rune' has multiple meanings; a rune can be an alphabetic character whose function is to record language or it could be a symbol of hidden meaning. The second suggestion finds its roots in the Old English definition of the word 'run', given directly as 'mystery' and 'secret'. This is supported by other languages that derive from the same source as Old English having a similar meaning for the word 'run' that relates to mysteries and secrets. Historians, or runologists debate the significance and meaning of runes, with some in favour of the theory that runes are nothing more than alphabetic characters, whilst others support the notion that runes are also symbols carrying special meanings. However, whilst we do know that runes are alphabetic characters used in northern Europe between 100 CE and 1300 CE, there are no definitive teachings in runology. There exists no official doctrine that records exactly what these Nordic runes are, or if there was then it is lost to time. What we believe to know about runes is largely educated conjecture, therefore we cannot discredit the use of runes as a method of divination. To understand the significance of runes, it shall be informative to explore the history of the existing rune sets.

Elder Futhark

The earliest recorded rune system is the Elder Futhark, and is the inspiration from which the other runic systems appear to evolve from. The name Futhark is derived from the first 6 characters, with the 24 runes being divided into 3 sets of 8, known as an 'aettir'. Each aettir is sacred to a God: Frey (or Freya), Hagal and Tyr. Its exact date of creation is not known, but is generally agreed amongst historians to be between 100 CE and 700 CE, with its origins placed in Germanic territories (Barnes, 2012).

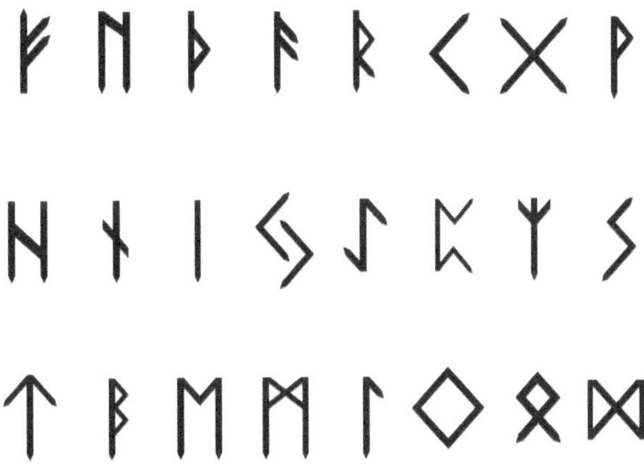

Figure 1. The Elder Futhark Runes arranged into their three aettirs.

Younger Futhark

The Younger Futhark rune system follows on from the Elder Futhark runes; it is believed to have been created in approximately 700 CE, in the Scandinavian region. The aptly named Younger Futhark runes consist of 16 characters and presents a simpler set of symbols. How these symbols appear differs slightly depending on the region they were used in. The Younger Futhark alphabet was eventually replaced by the Roman alphabet, effectively outlawing use of the Younger Futhark runes.

Anglo-Saxon Futhorc

The Anglo-Saxon Futhorc, alternatively known as Anglo-Saxon runes or Anglo-Frisian runes were used between approximately 450 CE and 1000 CE. Again, the exact origins are unknown, but it has been linked to the ancient northern European region of Frisia (modern day Netherlands and small parts of North Germany). It is an expansion of the Elder Futhark; the quantity of characters varies between 29 and 33.

Medieval Futhark

The Medieval Futhark, or Medieval runes as they are also known, then evolved from the Younger Futhark somewhere between 1000 CE and 1200 CE. Consisting of 27 symbols, it presents a more complex set of characters than its predecessor and it is thought that the runes evolved gradually over time (Barnes, 2012).

As ancient as the runes may be, the art of divination with runes as we know it is a relatively modern practice. Notably, Ralph Blum established a system of rune reading that he published in his 1982 book titled 'The Book of Runes'. Blum took an ancient, pre-existing alphabet and carved out a way to use it for divination. Using the runes, or any other oracle is an innately intuitive experience and there is no right or wrong way to do it. Often, when we practice divination for ourselves, we see what we need to see by projecting onto the abstract images in front of us, be that tarot cards, runes or tea leaves.

The beauty of runes is in presenting ourselves with an array of symbolic glyphs that we can use for spiritual guidance; the entire process of creating the runes is hands-on and personal. You are involved in selecting the materials, drawing the symbol and performing your own reading. Runes are small and tactile, and can be made from a variety of materials. Selecting each rune stone can be a journey of connecting with the energy that each symbol represents, making your final creation distinctively and exclusively yours.

What are the Witches' Runes?

The Witches runes present something of a tangled web at first glance, but their relative youth makes it easy to untangle if you have the patience to do so. The search for the earliest known published record leads us to Crystal Well, a magazine that began in 1965 as a series of occasional newsletters. Based in the USA, the publication developed into a quarterly instalment that focused on Neo-Paganism and earth based spirituality. In 1975 Crystal Well published an article about the Witches' Runes by Dana Corby. Corby is a practising witch who came to the craft in 1971 and was one of the founders of the Covenant of the Goddess. The article written by Corby was later expanded upon in a short book that was available via private distribution. This book was then released for sale to the general public as 'The Witches' Runes: A Traditional Divination System', and is still available today. However, the runes that Corby discusses are quite different from the Witches' runes that currently dominate the marketplace.

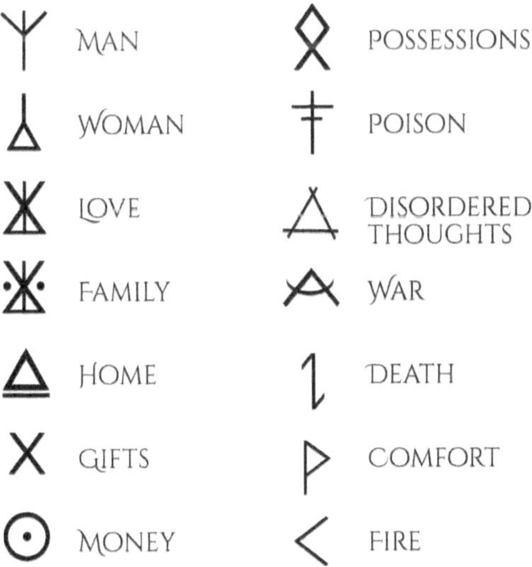

Figure 2. The Witches' Runes of Dana Corby

Consisting of fourteen rather than thirteen runes, they include symbols for Poison, Money, War, Gift, Possessions and Comfort. Five of the rune stones in this version are from the Elder Futhark, carrying the same symbolism but under a different name; those familiar with this runic system will recognise Algiz, Gebo, Othala, Eihwaz, Kenaz and Wunjo. The other symbols resemble the Elder Futhark in style but are from various sources. For example, the rune for Money is the astrological symbol for the sun.

Following on from Corby's work, we find a set of Witches' runes that resembles the 1975 version in name only, and is the inspiration for this publication. The creation of Susan Sheppard in her 1998 book 'Witch's Runes: How to Make and Use Your Own Magick Stones', Sheppard laments that witches do not have a divination system that is purely their own, encouraging her to create one by merging together Pictish symbolism with the zodiac. The Picts, sometimes referred to as 'the painted people', were a settlement whose name first appears in historical texts during the third century. Hudson (2014) explains that for 600 years, Scotland was their territory which they fiercely defended from Romans, Vikings, Anglo Saxons and the Southern British. The Picts left behind a legacy of art in the form of stone carvings and their pictographic alphabet made up of simple drawings. Much of what we know about the Picts comes from information that was recorded about them by their rivals, so they leave us with an air of mystery and intrigue. Sheppard's background in astrology served as the influence for the runic system she devised, consisting of twelve stones that correspond to the twelve zodiac signs, completed with a thirteenth rune that represents mystery. A pleasing total number of Runes, given the significance that the number thirteen carries in occult circles. It is the number of moon phases in the yearly cycle, as well as the number of Witches in a traditional coven. Although this specific set of runes is Sheppard's own creation, she intentionally chose symbols that hold a universal meaning. Appearing across various cultures, they allude to a divinatory language that exists within the collective consciousness. The eye, for example, is a symbol that frequently appears as a symbol of protection, watchfulness and omnipotence. This is quite logical really, as the eye stands out above all other organs as the primary source for receiving information. The Hamsa, or Hand of Fatima, a symbol that originates in the Middle East is an example of the eye being used as a protective amulet, notably as protection against the 'Evil Eye'. Turning our attention to the symbolism of the sun throughout time, it is common to see it as a symbol of growth and vitality. It is fascinating how the language of symbolism transcends time and cultural barriers, making it instinctual to understand.

Whilst the Witches' Runes are not ancient, they draw from an ancient well, tying together the common threads of human understanding in a compact system. Do not let the relative youth of this oracle deter you from embracing its magic.

Everything has to begin somewhere, and if it resonates with you then it has value. These simple symbols are drawn again and again by people with no connection to the other, simply because they are straightforward in conveying a message. As a form of folk divination, the ease at which one can learn to cast and read these runes makes them accessible to both novice practitioners and seasoned diviners alike.

The belief that something is ancient can make it seem alluring and mystical. Referring to a practice as 'ancient' can romanticise it, endowing it with a ceremonial element that reinforces its status as occult or magickal. Perhaps such a belief is the driving force that encourages some practitioners of the craft to engineer connections between their current practice and ancient practices, as a means to justify the relevance of a tool, ritual or system. To approach the craft without judgment though, means letting go of a need to justify the validity of how you operate. If you like the Witches' runes, then use them. Whilst ancient practices can indeed be worth treasuring, finding the magick in something new is immensely valuable too. Knowledge should not be static; to spiral outwards in an expansive manner means to always be learning something new or observing the world through a fresh perspective. Both Corby and Sheppard offered up their own runic creations, sharing their knowledge and artistry with those that wished to learn it. Now I share with you my own changing interpretation of the Witches' runes that brings a fresh dimension to the meanings. Perhaps in time you too will modify the meaning of the symbolism in a way that reflects your world-view. This is how folk systems develop; each person that uses it adds new layers of enchantment with every casting, because ultimately, the true power is in the heart of the practitioner, not the historical age of their apparatus.

When learning the Witches' runes myself, drawing connections between the zodiac symbols made it easy for me to grasp the archetypal energy that the runes represent. Overlapping the symbolism of the Moon rune with that of the astrological sign of Cancer made sense due to their shared connection to the element of water and the realm of emotion. The same can be said for friendly, passionate Leo as the embodiment of the Sun. However, some of the connections did not take root in my mind. Sheppard related Crossroads to the Saturnian energy of Capricorn, painting a picture of an inherently studious and severe rune. Be that as it may, I view each rune as having a dualistic polarity, occupying positive, negative and the spectrum in between. Crossroads can represent barriers and difficult choices, but it also conjures up the excitement of taking the path less trodden, of independently trailblazing in a new direction. The crossroads is a place of transition and potential, which I liken to the adventurous, free-spirited Sagittarius.

There is certainly a logical argument to be made for why Sheppard allocated the symbolism that she did; the expansive, generous energy of Jupiter (the ruling planet for Sagittarius) lends itself well to the Harvest rune for example. However, in place of Sagittarius, I have allocated Virgo to the Harvest because Virgo season coincides with the harvest season in the Northern hemisphere. The constellation of Virgo has ties to agricultural deities such as Demeter, the Goddess of the Harvest. This is not a critique of Sheppard, or a suggestion that she is wrong, it is merely an alternate perspective on the runes that is perhaps shaped by my own interest in Greek mythology. The inclusion of Greek mythology could be off-putting to those who do have any interest in it, but it should be noted that it is included in an archetypal sense, not a gnostic sense. The characters found in Greek myth are deeply ingrained in Western culture as thought structures, which I feel makes it easier to get a sense of the symbolism of the runes. In addition to this, the planetary symbolism that is so fundamental to astrology draws from Roman mythology, which absorbed Greek mythology, making it the obvious tie-in. The Witches' runes can be approached from an entirely secular perspective that does not require belief in a deity of any kind. In the chart shared here, I offer a breakdown of the associations I have given to each rune, along with Sheppard's interpretation to illustrate how the runes differ. Detailed explanations for the new interpretations are provided in the section that covers the meaning of each rune.

Witch Rune	Zodiac Sign (My interpretation)	Zodiac Sign (Susan Sheppard)	Planet Sign	Element
Sun	Leo	Leo	Sun	Fire
Moon	Cancer	Cancer	Moon	Water
Flight	Gemini	Gemini	Mercury	Air
Rings	Capricorn	Virgo	Saturn	Earth
Romance	Libra	Aries/Libra	Venus	Water
Woman	Taurus	Taurus	Venus	Earth/Water
Man	Aries	Aries	Mars	Fire/Air
Harvest	Virgo	Sagittarius	Mercury	Earth
Crossroads	Sagittarius	Capricorn	Jupiter	Fire
Star	Aquarius	Aquarius	Uranus	Air
Waves	Pisces	Pisces	Neptune	Water
Scythe	Scorpio	Scorpio	Pluto/Saturn	None
Eye	None/Yours	Yours	None/The Cosmos	Ether

How Runes Can be Used

Perhaps the primary use for Runes is in divination, but there are other ways to utilise them in your craft. A later chapter will go into detail on how to perform divination with the Witches' runes, but here we shall explore ways to incorporate them in spells and rituals too, using them as conduits for your energy that enhances the potency of your magick.

Candle Spells

A candle spell involves the dressing then lighting of a candle for a specific intention. The flame is lit as you sit with the fiery offering, directing your intention towards it. Perhaps you will anoint your candle with oils and herbs as you whisper an invocation to the universe. To imbue candle spells with additional layers of intent, consider carving one of the Witches' runes into the wax using a sharp implement. A toothpick or seam ripper are both helpful carving tools. The list below offers a guideline on how you could use the runes in your spells. Consider using one or more runes to express your intent in a more direct way. For example, Flight and Man both carry an assertive, direct energy so they could be combined with other runes when you wish to see fast results.

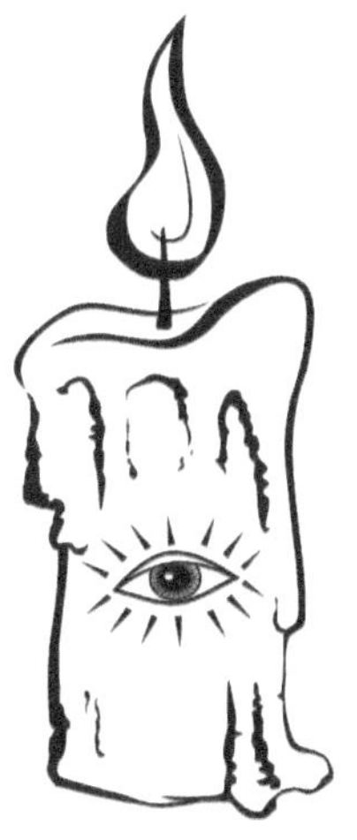

Harvest and Flight for example could indicate that you wish to scatter your seeds far and wide, whereas Woman and Romance might indicate that you are in no rush to develop friendships and are happy for them to form slowly and organically.

Witch Rune	Area of Spell craft
Sun	Confidence, passion, personal power, attracting attention, being charismatic, encouraging fast results, lust.
Moon	Enhancing intuition, soothing emotions, inviting in the next phase, encouraging prophetic dreams.
Flight	Study, focus, concentration, encouraging fast results, easy communication.
Rings	Co-operation, making new friends, expanding a community.
Romance	Love, friendship, harmony, creativity.
Woman	Healing, nourishment, reflection, introspection, soothing

	emotions, encouraging movement in a gentle manner.
Man	Standing up for yourself, being direct, being confident, projecting an idea outwards, confidence.
Harvest	Abundance, success, perseverance, encouraging maturity.
Crossroads	Guidance, help with choosing a path, opening the road ahead, inviting in adventure, embracing opportunity.
Star	Making a wish, asking for a blessing or protection, inviting in lucky energy.
Waves	Changing the direction of a situation, renewal, purity, cleansing, dissolving a barrier, connecting with deep emotions.
Scythe	Release, letting go, embracing the end, cord-cutting, preparing for a new cycle.
Eye	Protection, guidance, opening up your intuition, developing psychic abilities, warding against intrusion.

Talismans

A talisman is a small item that we create for a specific magickal purpose with a view to carrying it around with us. Talismans are symbols that embody our intentions and amplify our magickal workings, with jewellery offering us an almost unlimited opportunity for the creation of wearable talismans. Incorporate a rune of your choice onto a necklace, ring, earring, bracelet, belt buckle or brooch. A skilled wire-wrapper may be able to make something especially for you, but placing a drawing of the rune inside a locket could be just as effective. If you are creating the jewellery yourself, allow the process itself to be a ritual, keeping your focus in mind as you craft it. Talismans can also be placed in specific areas as a means to imbue a space with a certain energy. The Eye rune, for example, would lend itself well to being used as a talisman for home protection. Look to the materials around you for inspiration; a talisman could be as simple as drawing the symbol on a slip of paper then fixing it to the wall. If you're very creative you could fashion your talisman from clay, paint it onto a pebble or shell, or burn it onto a wood slice. You might place a Moon talisman near your bed to encourage visions in your dreams, or you may place the Sun rune by your mirror to encourage a glowing feeling of self-esteem.

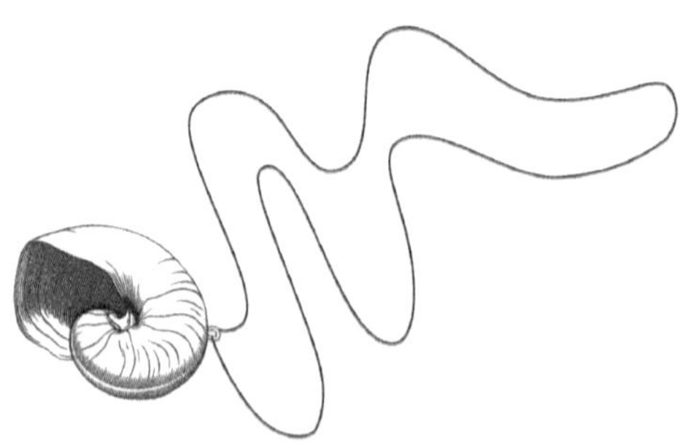

Sigils

Runes can also be used as sigils, abstract symbols that convey our ambitions and desires. Sigil is derived from the Latin word 'sigillum' meaning seal, with their use dating back to medieval times. A sigil can be created intuitively by drawing an abstract icon as you hold your aim in mind, but Austin Osman-Spare (1886-1956) is credited with devising a simple process that creates a sigil using the letter characters from the words of your intention to create a symbol that represents your desires in an abstract way. For example, if your goal was to attract love, you would use the characters 'L-O-V and E' to draw a symbol. The Osman-Spare method creates a link between your conscious and subconscious mind as letters are the language of consciousness, whereas symbols are the language of subconsciousness. Traditionally, sigils were burnt or destroyed after creation, operating on the basis that forgetting them consciously allowed them to take effect. However, some people prefer not to destroy their sigils, choosing instead to position them where they will be seen everyday.

The beauty of sigils as a form of spell craft lies in their simplicity; they require only pen and paper to create, and your artistic talents do not affect the success of your spell. The power of the Sigil is in the creation, a process personal to the individual. Once created, you may burn the paper it has been drawn on, carve it onto a candle, or draw it on your body using oils or make up. A sigil could be sewn into your clothing, drawn on the earth or written on the pages of a book. To use the Witches' runes as sigils you could combine one or more runes together, or choose a rune whose symbology matches your intent and draw it whilst holding that intent in your mind. You could even combine the freehand method of sigil creation with the Osman-Spare method by using the letters of a word to draw a stylised version of the Witches' rune of your choice.

Figure 3. A sigil created using the letters L, O, V and E.

Making your Runes

Creating your own Witches' rune set should be an enjoyable and intuitive process that lets you connect with the meanings behind each symbol as you etch or draw it onto your chosen canvas. The first decision to be made is the selection of the material for your runes. Choose something that resonates with you, or connects with your craft in some way. You will need thirteen small pieces on which to inscribe the symbols, taking into consideration colour, texture and elemental associations. Here are some suggested materials from which you can craft your runes, but don't be afraid to think outside the box and get creative with your runic base materials. If you obtain the materials for your runes from a natural place, consider leaving an offering. Your offering could be a song, an arrangement of flowers or leaves in a symbolic pattern, or an act of service such as litter picking. Offer something that expresses your gratitude to nature, without leaving behind any non-organic materials.

Wood Slices

Cut a fallen tree branch into thirteen small pieces using a saw, and smooth them off using sandpaper. The branch should ideally be 2cm to 4cm in diameter to make runes small enough to hold in the palm of your hand. Wood slices can be painted, drawn on, carved, or burnt into (pyrography). Wood is usually easily accessible in local parks or gardens, although it is best to use fallen branches rather than cutting pieces off of living trees. Obtaining the wood for your runes can be a special experience in itself. Perhaps you might make a pilgrimage to a forest location that holds special significance to you. Express your intent to find a branch for your runes, then wander through nature until you find a piece that feels right. Try to identify the type of tree that your branch has fallen from by matching it to the nearby trees. It will be interesting to know which type of tree has gifted you your runes. Different trees hold varying symbolism, providing you an opportunity to research tree folklore for the region. Although it isn't required, having such knowledge can deepen your connection to the runes you wish to create, making this an excellent option for people with an affinity to the element of earth. Once created, you can treat wooden runes by applying a wax based sealant.

Pebbles or Stones

Collect small, smooth pebbles from your local environment. Beaches and rivers are often the best place to find smooth pebbles that have had their rough edges worn away by the water. Choose small pebbles that have a flat enough surface for you to draw onto. Painting with acrylic paint or drawing with markers is the easiest way to make pebbles into runes, although they will require a top clear coat to preserve the image. Lay your stones onto greaseproof paper when you paint them. This way, when you turn them over to paint the reverse they are less likely to fuse to the paper.

Paint on a clear varnish as a top coat, or use a spray lacquer. Apply the clear coat in multiple, thin layers and allow it to dry fully between applications. Applying your clear coat as a spray rather than painting it on is usually preferable as the brush method can smudge the rune. Be sure to perform your painting in a well-ventilated area, away from open flames. Crafting your runes from pebbles lends itself well to people with an affinity to the element of water, providing the opportunity to discover folk tales attached to that specific body of water.

Sea Glass

Sea glass washes up from time to time on the shore; pieces of glass that have been transformed by the salty, turbulent waters into smooth, opaque coloured pebbles. You will have to be patient to collect thirteen pieces of sea glass as it is not the type of thing you find everyday. If you are lucky enough to be blessed with these pieces of ocean treasure then they would provide the ideal canvas for painting or drawing on. Do not carve sea glass in case it shatters.

Shells

Once again, look to the Ocean for runic inspiration. Any shell with a flat surface for drawing on will function as a rune. Ideas include clam shells, abalone, and sand dollars. Use markers or paint to draw on the smooth side of the shell, and apply a clear top coat to seal the image. Using sea shell runes might resonate with someone who identifies as a sea witch, drawing on the power of the ocean in their magical practice.

Glass Pebbles

Small, decorative glass stones that are readily available from craft stores make great, cost effective runes. Draw the symbols using a glass marker pen, then apply a top coat of sealant.

Crystals

Use thirteen uniform crystals, or collect thirteen different ones. You can carefully consider each crystal so that you select ones that have similar correspondences to the symbolism of the rune that they will represent. Here are suggestions to inspire you for each of the runes:

- Sun: Tiger's Eye, Citrine, Sunstone
- Moon: Moonstone, Opalite, Selenite
- Flight: Smokey Quartz, Snowflake Obsidian
- Rings: Pyrite, Unakite, Lapis Lazuli
- Romance: Garnet, Rhodochrosite
- Woman: Rose Quartz, Strawberry Quartz
- Man: Jasper, Carnelian, Hematite
- Harvest: Aventurine, Malachite
- Crossroads: Jade, Fluorite
- Waves: Sodalite, Aquamarine, Turquoise
- Star: Blue Lace Agate,
- Scythe: Onyx, Obsidian,
- Eye: Labradorite, Amethyst, Clear Quartz

Carving the runes into the crystals will require a power tool such as a dremel. Draw the rune on the surface first with a pen as a guideline, then carefully use the tool to trace your lines. You can fill in the rough grooves of the cuts afterwards with paint, to make the rune pop. Alternatively, you can paint the runes on, and apply a top coat of clear varnish. This is an advanced method of creating runes as using a power tool requires precision and skill. If you don't have experience in using such a tool, it would be advisable to find an experienced artist who can create a set of crystal runes for you. If you wish to go ahead with this method, find something to practice on before carving the crystals so you can refine your technique.

Clay

If you are particularly crafty, you can shape your own runes out of clay. A simple technique would be to roll your clay into a small ball, roughly 2cm in diameter. Flatten it by pushing it against a hard surface, then use a sharp tool such as a toothpick to push the image of the rune into the soft clay. Once it is dry, you can paint and varnish it. Drying methods depend on the type of clay used; some clays can air dry, whereas others need to be baked in an oven.

Practice drawing the symbols a few times before you create your runes. When you are ready to apply the glyphs to your chosen canvas, you can use permanent marker pens or acrylic paints. You can use oil paints too, but I have found that they take a long time to dry. Sealing your runes with a top clear quote will help provide durability.

Storing Your Runes

Once you have created your Witches' runes, you may like to store them somewhere special, such as a box or drawstring pouch. Select something that resonates with you, that will keep your runes safe from damage. If you have the skill to make a box, or sew a drawstring pouch that would certainly add a dimension of personalisation to your runes.

Consecrating Your Runes

When the process of creation is complete, you have the option of consecrating your runes, marking them as a sacred tool. How you choose to do this will be personal to you; here are a few ideas for consecration:

- Anoint them with a ritual oil. This could be something you have prepared yourself by diffusing herbs and crystals in oil.
- Anoint them with river or sea water. If your rune materials came from the water then this method may be most appropriate.
- Lay them in the moonlight. Choose a corresponding moon phase that has significance for you; the new moon or full moon are both brimming with symbolic power.
- Lay them in sunlight if solar energy resonates with you; be mindful of the material you have used as there is a risk of sun bleaching if they are left in the light too long.
- Cleanse them in sacred smoke. Burn incense, or herbs on a charcoal disk, then pass your runes through the tendrils of smoke, visualising them being cleansed of any residual energies.
- Light a candle. Lay your runes around the candle, visualising the light from the candle infusing the runes with energetic power.
- Sit with the runes in silent meditation; hold them in your hand, connect with them. Focus on how you wish to use them moving forward.
- Sleep with them underneath your pillow or by your bed so that the bond between yourself and the runes is strengthened in your unconscious state.

Reading the Runes

The beauty of the runes lies in their simplicity; when you wish to perform a reading, you simply cast a handful onto a smooth surface and interpret the symbols and formations that you see. However, whilst all readings usually begin with deciding on the purpose of the reading, there are various methods of interpretation open to the diviner, which we will discuss here.

Firstly, whichever method of casting you choose, begin by forming a clear question in your mind. This may be a request for guidance on a specific matter, or a desire for a general reading that delivers the message you need to hear at the moment. Try to approach a reading with a calm mind if you can; it helps to find a quiet place where you won't be disturbed so you may take a few slow, deep breaths as you think about your query. Once you feel as centred as you can, hold the runes between the palms of your hands before casting them gently. You can cast the entire set of thirteen stones, or just a small handful. No matter the method, once the runes have found their position in front of you, spend a few moments observing them without expectation. Let go of the pressure to immediately 'know' exactly what the spread means. Sometimes the need to perform an articulate, deeply spiritual reading can bring pressure and anxiety that interferes with your intuitive skills. Remind yourself that it is okay to be uncertain and allow yourself the time and space to slowly let the story unfurl before you. This reading is just for you; perhaps it challenges you in some way, but the more you practice casting the runes, the more comfortable you will become with interpreting the message they deliver.

A note on Positive and Negative Interpretations

In the pages dedicated to describing the symbolism of the stones, both positive and negative interpretations are made. This demonstrates the polarity of the runes which exist on a spectrum that encompasses the complexity of the human experience. Be mindful, that negative does not mean evil or bad, just as positive does not mean good and pure.

The cycle of life ebbs and flows in periods of heightened activity and lesser activity, so the meanings reflect this. Negative can mean dormant, passive or not relevant, whilst positive can suggest action, immediate movement or current relevancy. How you interpret the runes will depend on your personal reading style that will be unique to you. For example, if you cast all of the runes at once, some will inevitably fall face down. You must decide if the face down runes are not relevant to the reading, or if there is significance to them falling with the picture side down. Perhaps, if the rune falls face up, but the image is upside down, you may wish to interpret that as negative. When the runes land in a cluster, but some runes fall much further away from you, even if they are face up, you may view them as negative as they are distant from the other runes.

In a reading where all of the runes fall face up, you may intuitively know which runes carry a positive or negative message; that is the art of divination! There is no right or wrong way to make the distinction between positive and negative. Time will help you decide on your preferred reading style, as you bring your own flair to readings, forming a method that is as unique as your fingerprint. This book is a guide intended to help you along your path, it is not a doctrine that insists there is only one way to read the runes. As you grow in your practice, you may find that you interpret the rune meanings differently from how they are explained here. You are free to bring a fresh perspective to the symbols as knowledge should be a thing that continuously evolves, rather than a static unchanging set of principles. The way the rune symbols are explained in this book represents my own understanding of these virtually universal glyphs that exist within the collective consciousness. You may observe that the meanings in this book vary from others, as new layers of meaning are added.

Free Casting

Hold your runes in the palm of your hand, keeping your query in mind as you cast them onto a flat surface. Interpret the pattern of the runes before you, noticing which ones have fallen furthest from you and which are nearest. Runes that are positioned nearest to you may be read as having the most significant and immediate impact, in comparison to far away runes that may symbolize distant situations. Notice the flow of the runes; do they point downwards, upwards, or are they uniform? This could represent the energy flow in your life. Observe any clusters in the reading; runes that fall close together may have a connection or a strong impact on each other. Drawing upon the influence of planetary positions in astrology, three runes that land in an equal triangle formation may be working together to bring favourable energy, in contrast to runes that fall in an equal square formation which may present an obstacle or challenge. If two runes land parallel to each other at a distance from the main cluster, this could represent opposing factors that are having an influence on you.

Loop Method

The centre of the circle represents the heart of the matter, the outer edges represent your conscious thoughts and anything outside of the circle represents external influences.

EXTERNAL INFLUENCES

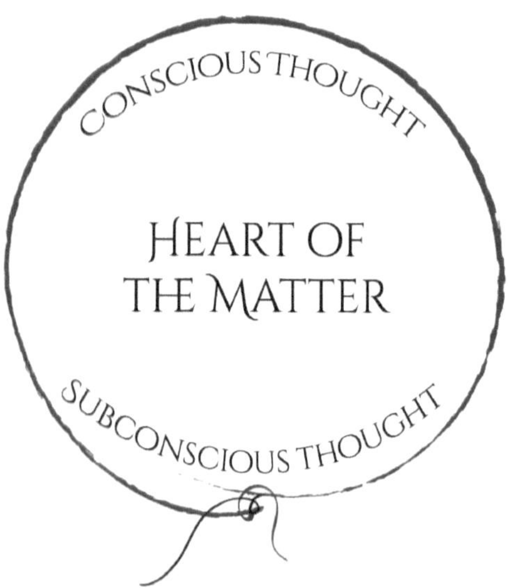

Obtain a piece of string approximately 3 feet long (1 meter). Tie the ends in a knot so you have a loop, lay it on a flat surface in the shape of a circle then cast your runes. This loop acts as a grid, defining the borders of the self, with the central point of the loop associated with the central focus of the reading, the heart of the matter or consciousness. Alternatively, the circle method can be read in a clockwise fashion, starting from the centre then up to the 12 o'clock position and around. This method is useful if you want to perform a 'time' based reading; each quarter of the circle could be seen to represent a segment of time. Whether you choose weeks, months or years depends on your requirements at the time of the reading. However, the common thread is that the circle's centre represents the reading's focus, whereas stones that fall outside of the circle represent outside influences, external factors or distant events. The stone that falls closest to the centre may act as the dominant stone for the reading, so that you may interpret the meaning of the other stones in relation to the central stone. Stones that fall close to the edge of the cord may represent things that are close to the surface of your consciousness, surface level thoughts. In contrast, stones that fall closer to the central stone may represent deeper subconscious thoughts. Interpret the stones, starting from the centre, moving directly upwards, then flowing clockwise around the loop. This is a highly intuitive practice whereby you should follow your gut instincts about the messages that jump out at you. As you read, you're creating a story with the stones, looking for patterns and ways to link them together. Let your subconscious be your guide as you look for meaning in the stones.

- The central rune represents the core focus of the reading.
- Rune stones that fall inside the circle represent the concepts that have the most immediate influence on the situation.
- When the stones fall outside of the circle, it can be symbolic of external influences outside of the self, or aspects that have little influence at present but may impact distant future events.
- The direction that the stone points can indicate the direction of its energy flow.
- Clusters of stones can reveal energies that are closely influencing each other.
- Start your reading from the centre, moving upwards towards the centre top of the string, then follow the stones clockwise around the loop, remembering to include stones that fall outside of the loop.

Rune Cloth

This method is similar to the free form casting, but instead the runes are projected onto a cloth with markings. These markings will designate particular areas of the cloth as symbolic of something, such as 'past, present and future', or 'subconscious and conscious'. This method may be easier to perform than free casting as the markings offer more immediate guidance. However, you will need to obtain a pre-made rune cloth, or design one yourself. Depending on your skill level, you can make your cloth using a plain dish towel and a fabric pen, or you could embroider one. Experiment with the following cloth designs, although you could read the runes by visualizing the layout if you feel comfortable remembering the designated sections:

Elemental Cloth

If you are familiar with the suits of the Tarot, then you may find you are already well versed in elemental symbolism. Divide your cloth like a compass for the four cardinal directions that represent an element, then place spirit in the centre, or divide your cloth into five sections that follow the points of the pentagram, placing spirit at the top point.

North (Earth): Runes that fall in earth signify matters relating to the home, body or finances. They indicate the practical and tangible aspects of life.

East (Air): Runes that land in air represent thoughts, beliefs and knowledge. They can also signify messages or advice.

South (Fire): Runes that land in fire indicate passions, desires and goals. The things that the querent feels most enthusiastic about. This area can also denote sexual desires.

West (Water): Runes that land in water symbolize emotions, feelings and intuition. This can be indicative of relationships that are familial, platonic or romantic.

Center (Spirit): This is optional, but you may wish to include a section for spirit or ether, the fifth element. This section would be designated for divine messages, or matters that relate to the querent's spiritual journey.

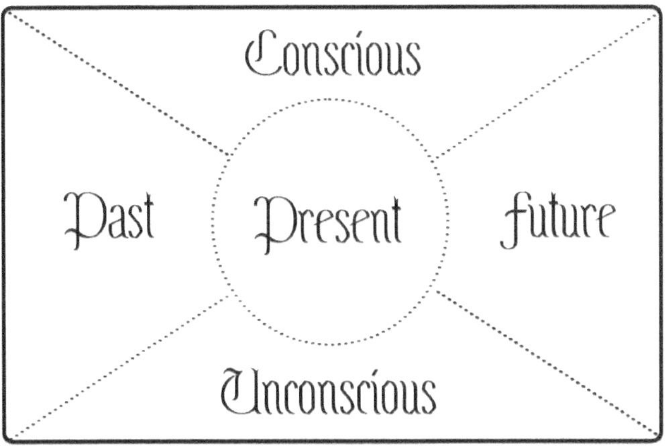

Past Present Future

This layout takes the form of a cross with 5 sections. The central area represents the heart of the reading, the present situation. If a rune falls on top of another rune, you may interpret this as an obstacle to the rune on the bottom. Runes that fall to the left of the central area indicate past influences, whereas runes that fall to the right represent future events and advice that the querent should act upon. Conscious thoughts, influences and beliefs held by the querent are signified by runes that fall above the central area, whereas the runes beneath denote subconscious feelings and fears.

The Witches' Runes

The Meanings of the

Witches' Runes

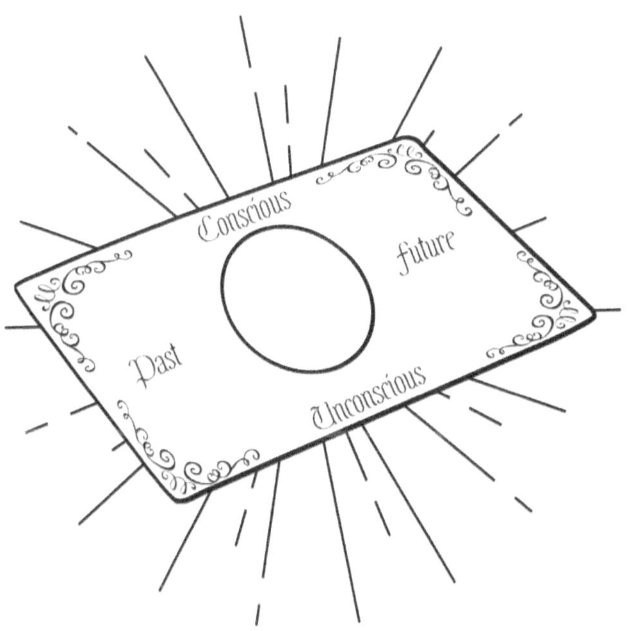

Sun

Keywords:
Warm, radiant, active, happy, confident, outer world, assertiveness, dominance, power, ego, outward personality, joy, pleasure, creativity.

Associations:
Element: Fire
Astrology: Leo
Deity: Apollo, Helios
Spirit Archetypes: Golden girl/boy, Ruler, The Hero, Monarch, Exalted self, Midas
Planet: Sun
Tarot Card: The Sun, Six of Wands, Strength

The brightest star in the sky, the centre of our solar system and the source of life on earth. Radiating warmth and light, it brings good health and vitality to all that its rays touch, making it the perfect symbol of golden days and happiness. It is a symbol of inherent joy; its appearance after a long winter is usually met with glee as its heat awakens the sleeping earth. Linked to the zodiac sign of Leo, illustrated by the Lion who stands proud with a mane as golden as the Sun itself. The lion is sometimes referred to as the King of beasts, reigning supreme in the jungle just as the Sun reigns in the sky. There is an air of regality to this fiery rune, representing the finer things in life and the aspects that bring us pleasure. The central vantage point of the Sun allows for a seamless metaphor to the centre of the self, or rather the ego. So brilliant as to be blinding, we can't help but see the Sun. It dominates the sky as it represents the things about us that others see, or our dominant traits. There is nothing hidden about the Sun, it commands attention and is often associated with a desire to be in the spotlight. As the source of all light, it is symbolic of the conscious mind and our public behaviour, along with the version of ourselves that we choose to show society. The Sun can only cast light on surfaces that are not obstructed; its rays do not penetrate the shadows. Essentially, it is related to what can be seen on the surface only. The Sun may be illuminating you to truth when it lands in a spread, the runes that it lands near are what is coming to light. Alternatively, the Sun rune may land nearby another to indicate that it is your greatest strength at this moment in time.

The direct, solar energy of the Sun is ambitious and assertive, going after what it wants with a self assured confidence of one's own power. It represents our drive for furthering ourselves and for gaining recognition for our achievements. It can relate to new beginnings and expansion as the sun is symbolic of growth and success.

It will most likely not come as a surprise that the Sun rune is associated with the actual Sun in astrology, sharing its symbolism with Apollo, the Greek God of music and prophecy. Beautiful Apollo is a shining and glorious figure associated with healing, vitality, creativity and the arts. He can also be counted within the pantheon of the original dragon/serpent slayers as he slayed the giant snake Python who guarded the temple at Delphi. Apollo is the hero who brings the light with his exuberant presence and passionate energy; the laurel wreath of victory became associated with him through the games he established at Pythia, showing a competitive edge to the God. There is some overlap too with Helios, the God of the Sun, but it is suggested that Helios is the manifestation of the Sun whereas Apollo embodies the essence of the Sun's energy, casting light and joy wherever he goes.

What it can mean in a reading:
The Sun may indicate the areas of our life in which we are going to experience growth and success, shining a light on where we have power to make change. This serves as a reminder that we will need to direct our energy to this particular area if we want the growth to remain consistent. Think of the Sun as a solar battery that charges you up with the stamina and strength to pursue your ambitions. There is a suggestion of stability for the moment too, as the Sun is a constant point in the solar system that isn't prone to retrogrades or cycles in quite the same way as other celestial bodies.

When the Sun appears in a reading it may be asking you to reflect on how you see yourself. For most humans, we are each the centre of our own universe to an extent, just as the Sun is the centre of our shared universe. Is your perception of the self accurate? If you often doubt yourself and your abilities, take stock of what you have accomplished and be proud of it. You might be surprised at how others see you, even if you lack confidence in yourself. The Sun brings with it a message that you have so much warmth to offer. You inspire other people with your strength and courage so you owe it to those around you as much as to yourself to acknowledge that you are enough. Avoid self-criticism; not only does it erode your personal esteem but it feeds into a cycle of unhelpful thought patterns.

The happy, joyful Sun might show up to express a very simple sentiment: have fun! There is no need to be so serious all the time; life is for living so take a break and do something you enjoy. Everyone needs their days in the Sun; it is good for the soul to get outside, breathe in the fresh golden air, and let the Sun kiss your skin (responsibly of course). Maintain the balance between work and play because it is easy to forget that rest and laughter are important.

As a symbol of light and consciousness, the sun can highlight what you are aware of, nudging you to question your level of understanding and examine whether there is more information that needs to be uncovered.. Are you as present as you can be or is your mind elsewhere? The appearance of the Sun rune can show you where you need to bring more attention in your life.

Symbolic of your personal power and driving force, the Sun can show you the core of your strength. It can illuminate for you the source of your greatest gifts, indicating which qualities you ought to embrace for maximum success.

The sun is not always about the self; it provides others with its golden light, suggesting that we question how we are helping others to shine. Are we standing in the spotlight of somebody else, hogging the limelight for ourselves? Perhaps we shine so brightly that we have a responsibility to light up the lives of those around us with our energy.

The Sun may appear when we have the golden touch; the outlook ahead looks positive for what we are trying to achieve, so act now. Be mindful though not to be greedy. If a golden touch transitions into a Midas touch then things can quickly go awry.

When negative:
Sun energy can manifest negatively as egotism, entitlement and tyrannical behaviour. The sun may provide the light and warmth that is essential to our survival, but too much heat leaves the land scorched and barren. If a person is too dominant and powerful they can become overbearing and dismissive of the needs of others. It is good to be confident and self-assured, but be mindful not to let this become hubris. Remember that pride comes before a fall!

Negative sun energy can suggest a person that is vain; so focused on the outer self that they neglect to look inwards to examine their thoughts and motivations. This can manifest as shallowness or arrogant, boastful behaviour. Alternatively, it may suggest a person who is out of touch with how they present themselves to others; perhaps they have no time for social graces and outward appearances. They may be perceived as coarse and unfriendly. A lack of confidence can also be suggested; somebody who has lost their spark and wants to avoid the spotlight at all costs. If you are afraid of receiving attention, explore why that is as you assess the ways in which this could be holding you back from progressing.

The Sun can represent things that are too dominant or over bearing. At first they may seem positive, but things quickly become uncomfortable when they are 'too much'. Examine whether you interfere much in the lives of others, and take into consideration the tendency to seek attention. Are you so determined to shine that you can't bear to see anyone else have their moment? The Sun can speak to self-centred behaviour that is so fixated on the self it robs you of empathy for others.

The unfavourable aspect of the Sun hints as shallowness, a superficial interest in others that is only concerned by good looks and status. Such a fixation robs you of developing relationships of any real depth. Conversely, the Sun could indicate a person who is petrified of allowing others to see the true them. Perhaps, born of a fear that they are lacking in some way, they uphold a golden mask so shiny and extravagant that it distracts people from ever looking beneath the surface. If you identify with this, then the Sun would remind you that you are magnificent inside and out, so let the mask slip from time to time.

Questions to ask when the Sun appears in a reading:
How focussed am I on outward appearances?
How do I see myself?
What do I like about myself?
Do I let others see beyond my surface level self?
Am I afraid to let myself shine?
How can I help others to shine?
Am I in touch with my personal power?
Do I make time for play?

Moon

Keywords:
Subconscious, emotion, inner self, hidden feelings, receptive, feminine, mysterious, fluid, passivity, intuition, nurturing, obsession, illusion.

Associations:
Element: Water
Astrology: Cancer
Deity: Artemis, Selene, Hekate
Spirit Archetype: Maiden, Mother, Crone, Dreamer, Mystic
Planet: Moon
Tarot Card: The Moon, The High Priestess

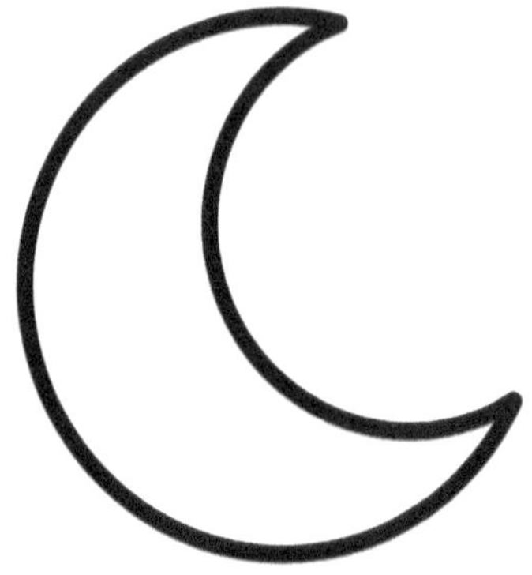

The Moon has a long standing connection with cyclical energy owing to its ever changing transition from waxing, to full, to waning. The Moon represents the subconscious; knowledge which dwells in the recess of our minds and may seem out of reach and confusing at times. It can suggest illusion or concealment. The association with our inner world makes the moon a symbol of intuition, inner knowing and sacred knowledge. Ever changing and cycling through phases, sometimes the moon's face is completely hidden during the New Moon stage. Consider also, that the other half of the Moon, the dark side, is always concealed from us. The Moon stands for everything that we don't see at first, things that take time to be understood. We cannot view the moon's fullness on demand, we must wait until the time is right, until the Sun illuminates it at just the right angle. It takes patience to observe the moon in all of its phases, just as it takes patience to look beneath the surface of our conscious thoughts and discover what dwells out of our reach. Again, we cannot look on demand, but must wait for subtle signs to emerge from our subconscious, giving us hints and clues about what is there.

There are many deities with ties to the Moon. Greek Goddess Selene is the embodiment of this silver orb, riding her chariot across the night sky from East to West. During one of her nightly journeys, Selene fell in love with a handsome shepherd sleeping on a hillside. The Goddess chose to have him placed in an eternal sleep which preserved his youth and meant she could visit him in his dreams forever-more. Artemis, the Goddess of the Hunt, could be seen to represent the wild aspect of the Moon. The full Moon has a reputation of enticing people into a frenzied state, and untameable Artemis who rejects the tradition of marriage in preference for living in the wilderness could be viewed as living perpetually in a state of undomesticated freedom. It is, after all, in the darkness of night that people put aside the tame self so that they may unleash their primal side.

Next we must look to the Titan Goddess Hekate who holds connection to the crossroads as well as the Moon. Hekate is sometimes attributed with the waning moon, giving her a crone aspect. She is wise, benevolent and fair, offering guidance to those in need. The shifting, ephemeral edges of Hekate make her difficult to define, but this is the embodiment of the Moon's nebulous energy that continually shifts in its cycle. Hekate is the keeper of keys, a guardian of knowledge who will only grant you access when the time is right.

Symbolic of intuition, the Moon represents the innate knowledge we have that guides us onto the best path for us at the time. When we experience a flash of intuition, it may manifest as a 'gut feeling', a fluttering, stirring in the stomach region. The Moon calls us to trust this feeling; there may be no physical evidence of foul play, nothing that can be seen on the surface, but an instinctive inner knowing tells us to be aware. In these instances, we trust what we know, not what we see. This is part of the Moons mystique; we may not always understand its ways, but we know when to listen to its guidance.

The Moon and water have a close connection; the Moon influences the ocean tides, causing them to rise and fall, ebb and flow. This watery connection explains the Moon's kinship to the domain of feeling and emotion. Our emotions are not always visible on the surface; we experience a huge spectrum of feelings and many of those may be concealed from outside eyes. Emotions are not static, they shift and change. Just like the water they are linked to, emotions can quickly transition from calm and placid to turbulent and choppy.

What it can mean in a reading:
The Moon can indicate the areas of your subconscious mind that need attention. It shows what is hidden beneath the surface and asks you to go inwards and look a little deeper. It may be the thread of a shadow behaviour that is subtly making itself known to you. Spend time in introspection so that you can shed some silvery light on what memories or old habits are lurking in the depths of the mind.

When the Moon appears in a casting, it may be asking you to explore, or connect with your feelings relating to a specific subject. Look to the surrounding rune clusters for an indication of what these areas might be. Rather than taking a definitive action, the Moon rune counsels examination of your emotional state before making any rash decisions. Sometimes we get so caught up in acting or doing, we forget to feel in to the heart of the matter.

The Moon may be asking you to adopt a more flexible, fluid or cyclical attitude towards certain key areas of your life. Open your mind to ideas that may seem a little 'outside of the box' and don't be afraid to step off the path most travelled from time to time. The Moon transitions through a continual cycle of waxing and waning which speaks of new phases as well as the ebb and flow of energy. This, coupled with the Moon's connection to water, can be a reminder to adopt a more fluid attitude and go with the flow.

The appearance of the Moon might be a call to take a more passive approach to a situation. Rather than rushing in and taking direct action, employ subtler, gentle tactics. Use patience and understanding. It may be a slow process, but could pay off in the long term.

The Moon is synonymous with mystery and magic, representing the allure of the unknown. Only ever showing half of its face, the dark side of the Moon is always concealed, encouraging us to retain a little bit of mystery. The appearance of the Moon rune may be an indication that a little magic is needed. Perhaps it is time to stop over-analysing and instead allow yourself to be overtaken with wonder. You may be dealing with a situation that can't be solved with logic. Some things are unknown and perhaps they are meant to stay that way. On the other hand, you may feel more in tune with your environment if you stop resisting the lunacy and just flow with it. You might even find it fun after all.

The Moon could be a call to trust your intuition. Listen to those inner feelings; the more attention you give to that inner voice, the more connected you will become with your innate intuitive abilities.

When Negative:
On the negative side, lunar energy can manifest as moodiness, irrationality and anxiety. It can be confusing and illogical, relying on feelings and emotions rather than facts. It can also represent failing to take action when direct action is necessary.

The Moon may point to the things that are being kept hidden from us. Perhaps this is a deliberate deception, or maybe we are just not ready to hear the truth of the matter. When the Moon appears in a reading consider whether you really have all of the information and perhaps hold off on making a decision until you know more. If you only know part of the store it will be difficult to make a fair choice. Hidden information also points to illusion. Things may not be as they seem so tread cautiously.

When unfavourable, the Moon can signify mental unease. Resistance to the 'ebb and flow' fluidity of lunar energy may manifest as stagnation or obsession. Perhaps we are fixated on something or someone from the past, and holding onto a fantasy causes us to be stuck in a situation that doesn't allow for personal growth. It could be that we prefer to live in a fantasy world and reject the real world, retreating into the comfort and safety of our own illusions. Think of Selene, locking her lover in an everlasting dream rather than conducting a real-life relationship with him. Embracing the highs and lows of life is a part of the human experience; shunning reality denies us the chance to experience the magick that is waiting to be discovered.

Periods of disconnection from reality and failure to take care of your mental health are manifestations of negative lunar energy. The word 'lunacy' is derived from the Latin word lunaticus and implies temporary madness caused by the Moon. In a rune reading, the appearance of the Moon can imply a person is acting without rationality or they have become too detached from reality.

Questions to ask when the Moon appears in a reading:
What aspects of myself do I intentionally conceal?
What is being hidden from me?
Do I feel able to follow the natural rhythms of life?
Do I have the patience to gather more information before making a decision?
Do I trust my intuition?
What do I obsess over?
What are my deepest fears?
Am I honest about my feelings?
Do I handle my feelings in a healthy manner?
When do I prefer fantasy to reality?

Flight

Keywords:
Travel, transport, freedom, communication, language, intellect, planning, logic, fast paced, truth, stubborn, deceptive, fickle, restless energy.

Associations:
Element: Air
Astrology: Gemini
Deities: Hermes/Mercury
Spirit Archetypes: Messenger, Traveller, Trickster, Rebel, Intellectual, Philosopher
Planet: Mercury
Tarot Card: The Magician, Ace of Swords

The Flight rune depicts birds in travel, soaring through the air. Travel and journeys, both literal and spiritual are suggested by Flight. It indicates swift movement that is free from obstacles, whilst the airy nature of flight is synonymous with thoughts, the intellect and communication. It speaks to having the freedom to take the path that calls to you, as well as messages and communication styles. Just like the carrier pigeons of a bygone era, these birds might be arriving to deliver you an important message. Look to surrounding runes for a suggestion of what news is being carried to you on the wind.

We could liken this rune to the Greek messenger God Hermes who was known for his sharp intellect, deceptive nature, and skill at communicating. His winged sandals allowed for swift movement, making him the messenger to the other Gods. Capricious and fickle, you never know which face Hermes will show as his nature can flip as suddenly as the wind changes. In a sense, there is a neutrality to Hermes as he doesn't belong to either 'side'. To view Flight as a conduit for the mercurial energy of Hermes, we may see it as indicating that we must use all of our ingenuity and intellect in order to deliver a compelling argument. Perhaps we need to channel the trickster archetype in order to devise a clever way to reach our goals. This calls for research and tactical planning that draws on the intellectual nature of this rune.

As a rune of the mind, we may be called to transcend the rational, analytical mind so that we may enter the plane of higher consciousness. Higher thought is needed; take time to nurture your spirit by meditating and reflecting upon what you know. Whilst using the intellect in a mundane sense to achieve your earthly goals will benefit you in the short term, there is an awakening that can be achieved when you view the universe as interconnected.

What it can mean in a reading:
When Flight appears in a reading, it can relate to movement and travel in a literal way, suggesting that swift action ought to be undertaken or journeys embarked upon. Whilst swiftness of movement is implied, it could also refer to swiftness of the mind. Perhaps you are being called to use your intellect to solve a problem. When faced with an obstacle, take a logical approach by carrying out research to form a well thought out plan of action. Maybe you need to be strategic, or employ cunning to find loopholes or exploit weaknesses to your advantage. Consider the saying that 'the pen is mightier than the sword' and understand how knowledge is a great strength. Seek to diffuse tension with words of reason and a subtle application of human psychology rather than aggression and dominance.

Flight invites you to think about how you communicate with the world; do you express yourself authentically? Articulating your thoughts and opinions effectively is a skill worth investing in because it is time to speak up and state your truth! The birds of Flight sing out free and clear, and they encourage you to do the same. Do not silence your voice any more. Perhaps you need to examine your beliefs to become familiar with what they are before you put them into words. Poor communication can have disastrous consequences upon friendships, romantic relationships and jobs. Maintaining an open avenue of clear, honest communication can go a long way to diffusing problems that occur. Give careful thought to your endeavours; form alternate plans and do not rest on your laurels. When decisions need to be made, this rune advises you to think with the head and not the heart. This is not the time to be led by emotions, nostalgia or feelings. Take a logical, pragmatic approach and put your own bias aside.

The free and unrestrained nature of Flight could be a sign that you ought not to commit to the first thing that comes along, whether that is a job, relationship or ideology. Remain neutral, impartial or fluid, occupying the role that fits you best at any given time. Now is not the time to ground yourself by committing to something that would place a heavy burden upon you. Be wary of over-committing your time as you endeavour to hold on to your freedom. If you can keep the avenue open to transition between different roles as they suit you, it will open you up to enjoying a richer, more complex human experience. Flight could appear when you feel restless and confined by your present circumstances, suggesting a need to break free so that you may move on to the next chapter of your life. In this way, Flight could represent the moment in which you leave behind the old ways. Be prepared to go with the flow, and question anything that demands rigid conformity.

When Negative:
When Flight is interpreted unfavourably, a lack of knowledge or understanding could be suggested; approach this as an opportunity to explore a topic further and increase your awareness of a given subject. Be mindful that you are not on the receiving end of another's manipulation or fraud, being wary of things that seem too good to be true. As the emblem for the trickster archetype, the appearance of this rune may be a warning to keep your guard up around smooth-talking individuals. Be wary also, that you are not the one who is being unethical in your manipulation of others. Manipulative tactics can have their advantages, but be strategic about how they are applied.

Flight may ask you to examine if you are communicating skilfully enough to be heard. If you find yourself being ignored or misunderstood, delve into your communication style and consider alternative ways to interact and get your point across. Perception styles are unique, so consider how you may need to modify your message depending on who you are talking to. A 'one size fits all' approach may not be the best way to convey information. Speak up, and let your voice travel upon the air.

The wind on which the birds of flight soar can change in an instant. Fickle and unpredictable, it might not blow in the direction that you hope for, suggesting erratic, scattered energy. Take a step back and analyse how you are managing your time. If there is no structure or logic to your day to day life then you may find that you are draining yourself with unnecessary or repetitive tasks. Take time to place your focus on what really matters and step away from needless distraction. Ask yourself, 'is it necessary'? Remove mental clutter from your day so that you give your time and energy to what really matters to you. Form a plan in order to bring a sense of direction to your life. Whilst the best laid plans do not always unfold as we wish they would, having purpose and direction aligns you with your desires more effectively than a disorderly approach. Conversely, Flight may imply that you have become too rigidly fixated on something in particular, and it is preventing you from seeing things clearly. Perhaps logic is preventing you from using intuition, keeping you too grounded to think bigger. Or maybe you are soaring so high in the upper realms of spirituality that you have lost touch with physical reality. Any type of imbalance will have negative consequences, suggesting a need to walk the line between the intellect and the inner knowing.

The intellectual aspect of Flight is hungry for information; this is generally a good thing but be wary of collecting too much 'surface level' information without delving any deeper into a subject. It is likely to be more beneficial to study one topic in detail than five or six at a basic level. Take a deep dive into the subjects that interest you, and process them fully before jumping to the next topic. The restless nature of this air-based rune can be easily distracted, so find a way to concentrate on one thing at a time before starting on the next project.

Questions to ask when Flight appears in a reading:
Where do I want to direct my time and energy?
What places do I feel drawn towards?
In what ways do I feel that my freedom of movement is restricted?
Am I an effective communicator?
Which areas of my life could benefit from an analytical approach?
Are there subjects on which I have expertise?
Do I manipulate others to meet my own needs?
Are there times that I have been manipulated or deceived?
Which areas of my life would benefit from a tactical approach?
Am I confident in my ability to express myself clearly?
Do I put my own needs first?
Do I hold biased views which may be limiting to my growth?
Am I swift to act when the situation calls for it?
Do I operate from a place of logic, or a place of emotions?
Can I diffuse tension with soothing words?
Am I spending my energy wisely?

Rings

Keywords: Promises, contracts, commitment, union, community, partnerships, sacred vows, merging of opposites, creativity, pragmatism.

Associations:
Element: Earth
Astrology: Capricorn
Deities: Hephaestus
Spirit Archetypes: The Inventor, Leader of an Organisation, The Sustainer
Planet: Saturn
Tarot Card: The Hierophant

The Rings, whether represented by two or three intersecting circles, hold the same meaning. They are not mere geometric shapes but potent symbols of eternity, sacred vows, and promises made. The ring, in its circular form, represents the cyclical nature of existence, the endless journey of life, death, and rebirth. It symbolizes the unending nature of love, commitment, and the interconnectedness of existence.

Unlike the romantic and spiritual unions associated with the Romance card, the Rings hold a more pragmatic and practical symbolism. They represent the coming together of individuals or entities to achieve a common goal. It signifies the merging of energy, resources, and intentions to work towards a shared purpose. While there is an element of partnership within the Rings, it is distinct from the passionate and emotional connection of Romance.

Being connected with the stoic planet of Saturn which rules over hard-working Capricorn, the Rings also hold a sense of bureaucracy and established order. They represent the structures and traditions that govern relationships and communities. In the context of marriage, for example, the love shared between two individuals may be deeply spiritual and emotional, but the act of making wedding vows introduces a contractual element. This contractual aspect requires the involvement of an external body, such as a religious or legal authority, to sanction and legitimize the union.

The Rings encompass the practical realities and responsibilities that accompany long-term commitments. They symbolize the need for compromise, negotiation, and the balancing of individual desires with the needs of the collective. While the rings represent the union of two or more individuals, they also highlight the importance of maintaining one's autonomy and identity within the partnership.

The Rings serve as a reminder that relationships require dedication, effort, and a willingness to work together towards a common vision. They represent the intricate dance between the individual and the collective, the spiritual and the practical, and the eternal and the temporal.

Hephaestus, the Greek God of the forge shares a similar energy with this rune. Primarily, as a blacksmith, golden rings are exactly the type of thing that he would create in the smouldering fires of his workspace. Hephaestus was an artisan, a deeply creative deity who crafted objects of exquisite beauty for the other Gods including the winged sandals of Hermes and the breastplate of Athena. Although creative, Hephaestus held others accountable for their actions by punishing them for neglecting their obligations. For his mother Hera, who mistreated him as an infant, he sent a magical chair that bound her to it, and for his wife Aphrodite who had a love affair with Ares, he trapped her in an unbreakable net. Not known for his strength, Hephaestus used a combination of artistic skill and thoughtful planning to achieve his aims. This is shown in the symbology of the rings, as ideas merge and mingle to bring forth creative solutions.

What it can mean in a reading:
When Rings appear in a reading it can indicate a desire to dedicate yourself wholly to something. This could be a person, place or job, and it suggests that either you or the other party might require protection in the guise of a formal agreement. In this sense, the Rings might be here to advise you to read the small print. Have a clear understanding of what is expected of you, even if this is just a verbal agreement where each party defines their expectations. It can indicate initiation into a closed community that requires a level of commitment before they accept you into the fold, as well as representing organisations that hold a traditional structure. Such tradition could imply that there is a 'status quo' that must be maintained if everything is to flow smoothly. Whether you are making a promise to yourself or to another, Rings would advise you to stand by your word.

Defining your boundaries is a concept that can be expressed by Rings. In order to protect yourself and your energy resources you must have a clear threshold of what you are able to tolerate and what you will not. Rings invite you to be clear on where your edges lie so you don't continually push yourself beyond your means or lose yourself in the identify of another.

The overlapping of the Rings paints a picture of the merging of opposites that encourages you to get creative; energy combines and integrates to bring about transformation and union. This could be the alignment of the shadow with the conscious self or the union of mind and spirit. When unification is achieved, then expansion of higher consciousness can begin. It represents the quest for enlightenment and new growth, along with the creative power that one holds when they operate in alignment with their most authentic self. Rings can also represent polar energies that shine a light on each other; people working together harmoniously because they both bring different skills to the table.

Whilst we can view Rings as outside forces coming together, we could also see it as expansion if we regard it as a cell that duplicates itself over and over. From this perspective we might view it as a sociable rune that represents branching out, networking and forming a community. Perhaps it is time to find a community of people that align with your personal ethos, or maybe you are being called to build a community yourself.

When Negative:
The Rings can represent restrictions and boundaries that are too repressive. Examine your personal boundaries so that you may consider if they are serving you, or constraining you. Try to find the balance between protection and inhibition. Being too rigid in your way of thinking can prevent you from branching out.

Codependency is also suggested by the Rings; relying too heavily on the rules laid out by others can rob you of your sense of individuality. Whilst community can benefit us greatly, we still have to hold on to our ability to confidently make decisions for ourselves. A community should be a support network, but be mindful about handing too much of your personal power over to others.

The Rings can also warn against conformity that stifles you and extinguishes the essence of who you are. Be wary of becoming too wrapped up in the ways of an organisation or group. Rings could be a warning against becoming involved in cultist organisations. A warning sign to be mindful of is someone that tries to separate your other relationships and connections, causing you to be overly reliant on the community.

If you are experiencing a blockage in your creative flow, Rings may be asking you to examine the source of the block. Are you too concerned with how others may judge you to be able to create anything authentic? Fear of outside influence may be binding your creativity so try to separate yourself from pressure and expectation placed upon you by others.

Rings may be a reminder to share with others rather than holding on too tightly to what you feel is yours. Society flourishes when we share and support others, so be empathetic and kind to others. Grasping on too tightly to something can be limiting and restrictive.

Questions to ask when Rings appears in a reading:
What am I dedicated to?
What promises do I hold sacred?
Have I broken any vows or promises?
In what ways am I codependent?
Do I feel like I am a part of a community that supports me?
What could I do to branch out beyond my comfort zone?
Who do I work well with?
How could I form a beneficial partnership?

Romance

Keywords:
Love, harmony, fertility, self love, friendship, compassion, desire, confidence, attraction, passion, relationships, synergy

Associations:
Element: Water
Astrology: Libra
Deities: Aphrodite/Venus
Spirit Archetypes: The Lover, Companion, Soul Mate
Planet: Venus
Tarot Card: Temperance, Two of Cups

As the name suggests, Romance represents the relationships that consume us. This can be the burning, passionate desire felt for a romantic partner, or a platonic friendship based on shared ideals. It indicates that you are in the company of kindred spirits, the tribe of people that fill your life with joy, laughter and belonging. Emotional connections are signified by Romance, indicating the people, places or things to which we have a strong sense of attachment.

The Romance rune holds the energy of the Greek Goddess of Love and Beauty, Aphrodite (or her Roman counterpart Venus). She rules over beauty, love, desire, procreation and prosperity. However, there is a duality to Aphrodite in that she is known as 'Aphrodite Ourania', signifying a heavenly aspect that could be related to spiritual love, and Pandemos, meaning 'for all the people'. We could view this as the higher and lower octaves of love, of transcendent love in comparison to physical desire. Like a divine artist, Aphrodite is capable of blending, mixing and unifying elements harmoniously. For this reason, we could divide Aphrodite's sphere of influence across two of the Witches' runes, just as she rules over the two astrological signs of Libra and Taurus. Romance becomes symbolic of the Libran, heavenly Aphrodite Ourania whilst the Woman rune embodies the Taurean, earthly aspects of love, such as lust, luxury and pleasure.

When we speak of loving relationships and partnerships, we may see this as a union between two, but the symbol for Romance is a three-petaled flower that resembles a form of triquetra. A triquetra is an ancient symbol that has meant many things to different people across time and space, but is often used to symbolise groupings of three, known as trinities. Such trinities could be the three faces of a deity such as 'the father, the son and the holy spirit' that we see in a Christian context, or the modern pagan interpretation of the 'maiden, mother and crone'. In addition to triple aspects of a divine figure, it could also symbolise the harmonious union between realms, such as 'sky, land and sea'. Other notable trifectas include 'mind, body and soul' as well as 'life, death and rebirth'. The power of three that we can interpret from this beautiful symbol speaks to love that resonates on a deeper level. It is more than a shared bond between two, it is a harmony between multiple people. It is cooperation, tranquillity and peace, all merging together with no beginning or end. It is a selfless love as it does not wish to possess or confine as well as the creative force that emerges as a result of union.

What it can mean in a reading:

Romance can represent the energetic essence of synergy, the harmony that arises when people work together in tandem to produce something that is 'greater than the sum of the parts'. Synergy could be considered magic; the right people coming together at the perfect moment to create something spectacular. Each holds a talent of their own that is magnified and enhanced considerably when they combine forces with the other. Look to the surrounding runes for an indication of where you can find or create the greatest amount of synergy in your life.

When Romance shows up in a reading it can be a call to bring a spark of light into the mundane, reminding us to find wonderment, beauty and joy where we can. Beauty ought not to be limited to the ideals of impossible perfection because it is subjective to the beholder. Our perception of another's beauty can be transformed by a radiant smile or an infectious laugh. Beauty is not just on the outside; it shines from within when we allow ourselves to be curious and joyful. Romance invites you to literally romanticise your life; colour your world with the things that spark joy and make life exciting. Ask yourself, what are you passionate about? What inspires you and fills you with enthusiasm? Romance points towards the things we find most fulfilling on a soul level, not just relationships. It might be time to discover what lights you up so that you may live a life you're excited for.

Romance may indicate that a new love is coming your way; a romantic partner or perhaps even a friend that you experience a deep connection with. A person that shares a common desire with you, or someone who brings joy and happiness into your life. This person, or group, will have a profound influence on you, helping you to grow and prosper as you expand your world-view. However, Romance can also be a reminder to express gratitude for what we have. It is easy to take things for granted, but the transitory, fleeting nature of existence is what makes our lives special. Take a moment to meditate on all that you are grateful for, considering how you could let someone know that you care about them. Nurture the relationships that you already have by making time for the people in your life. You don't need to make extravagant gestures, simply giving someone your full attention and taking an interest in their life can be enough to make someone feel valued. Check in with family members or reconnect with old friends.

Romance can indicate a deep fascination for something; look to the surrounding runes for an indication as to where a person's priorities and loyalty lies.

When Negative:
On the negative side, Romance can manifest as envy, greed and a desire to possess. Rather than building bridges, it builds walls, to jealously guard what it wishes to protect. In this sense, love is experienced selfishly, rather than shared as the focus is on how the self feels.

Romance can imply that you are not taking into consideration the feelings of others, particularly when they express them to you. A stubbornness coupled with a refusal to compromise is suggested, and this is causing disharmony and dissatisfaction in those around you. This rune may be asking you to shift your focus away from how you feel so that you may consider the effects that your behaviour has on others. Romance may appear when you are taking your relationships for granted, failing to nurture them as adequately as they require. On the other hand, it could suggest that you are trying too hard to please others, and your actions are not appreciated; be mindful too that excessive people pleasing can make a person vulnerable to being taken advantage of.

Romance might bring with it the message that no matter how hard you try, there is no way to turn this situation into a synergistic one, so you may be better off stepping away from a painful set of circumstances. Rather than the magical alchemy of synergy, you may find that the particular grouping of people brings out the worst in each other by agitating one another, or being too fearful of judgment to be authentic. Rather than sharing and inspiring, people are grasping selfishly for their own gain, consumed by self-need rather than the needs of the group as a whole.

If Romance can indicate a new relationship, then it can also express the yearning for love that goes unrequited. A desire left unfulfilled can cause us immense agony. If you're experiencing a period of heartbreak, take time to nurture yourself so that you may heal. Reach out to your support network of friends and family, and find space so that your inner harmony may be eventually restored.

Questions to ask when Romance appears in a reading:

When considering my personal relationships, which ones bring me joy and which ones cause me pain?
Do I make space for harmony and playfulness in my life? If not, how can I connect with the world in a pleasurable way?
What am I most enthusiastic about?
Do I cooperate well with others?
What am I holding on too tightly to?
Which of my relationships require more nurture?
Do I appreciate beauty in the world?
How can I romanticise my life?
Do I give others my full attention when they are speaking?
Are there times that I am too focused on how I feel, at the expense of others?

Woman

Keywords:
Yin, creative, receptive, reflective, introspection, fertility, nurture, beauty, compassion, unconscious, motherhood, Goddess

Associations:
Element: Earth/Water
Astrology: Taurus
Deities: Aphrodite/Venus, Demeter
Spirit Archetypes: Goddess, Mother figure, Mother Nature, Mystic
Planet: Venus
Tarot Card: Empress, Ace of Cups, Ace of Pentacles

The Woman rune represents the female principle in a conceptual sense. As an expression of energy, it embodies the polar opposite of the Man rune. Although the Woman and Man runes can signify a person, they can also represent the polarities of symbiotic energy, of stillness and action, passivity and assertiveness. If you prefer, you may think of these two runes as representatives of Yin and Yang, the philosophical concept of cyclical energy that occupies opposing yet complementary realms. It is a misconception that Yin and Yang represent the binary; yin and yang merge into each other in a fluid fashion, blending and unifying in a cosmic cycle. There is a little bit of Yin inside the Yang, just as there is Yang inside the Yin. The simple line drawing of the Woman rune could be seen to represent a chalice or cup. If you are familiar with the tarot then you will be aware of the symbolism of the cup, a vessel that is symbolic of emotion and love. The cup is a receptacle that is ready to be filled; bursting with potential, it holds the liquid that it receives within its depths. Such a notion can represent the womb that receives the seed, or the soul that receives divine inspiration. The cup holds space, providing a safe haven of comfort for those that seek it.

The Woman rune is symbolic of beauty, abundance, ripeness and fertility. Fertility can refer to the fruition of ideas and projects, and is not limited to the idea of birth. Your labours will pay off and you will find success in your creative ventures. This rune emanates an "Earth Mother" energy, reflecting a deep connection with nature and an appreciation for the material comforts the earth provides. It represents individuals who find solace and joy in immersing themselves in the beauty of the natural world, revelling in the simple pleasures it offers. The Woman is loving and nurturing and encourages you to manifest beauty in the world around you by tending to the things that light up your soul. There is a sexual undertone to this rune too, because the Woman is linked to new life and pregnancy. We can draw a similarity to Aphrodite from this rune. Where Romance embodies the higher, spiritual realms of love, Woman represents the earthly, physical side to the Goddess of Love and Beauty. Not only does Woman represent sensual pleasure and joy, she encourages the indulgence of the physical senses, luxuriating in opulence, comfort and high-living. Woman wishes us to experience all of the pleasure that our earthly senses allow, whether that's the intoxicating scent of a favourite perfume, a tantalizing meal or a night of intimacy with a lover.

What it means in a reading:
Being emblematic of passivity and receptivity, when Woman appears in a reading it can suggest there is no need to rush; take your time and move slowly as what you need will eventually come to you. Governed by the zodiac sign of Taurus which is strongly linked to the material and earthly matters, Woman suggests that all of your physical needs are met so there is no immediate call to action. Instead, you may express gratitude for all that you have. If there is something you wish to attract, the Woman advises that the best path is to let it come to you. Warm, open body language that doesn't grasp or demand attention might be the best way to subtly draw something into your orbit. The soft, placid nature of Woman advises you to turn inwards so that you might give thought and consideration to a situation before acting. Do not act in haste, instead give thought to the long term consequences and implications. There is a tendency to underestimate the power of softness, but there is immense power to be found in tenderness.

The energy of the Woman rune could be advising you to nurture and cultivate a particular area of your life. Relish your creativity as you gently tend to the needs of a project, goal or idea with kindness and compassion in order to see growth and development. Take a calm approach, removing expectations of sudden or immediate change. Being linked to the realm of emotion and intuition, Woman may be encouraging you to think with the heart rather than the head. Logic may dictate that a certain path is the sensible option, but perhaps you feel called in another direction by an instinct that you can't explain. Trust this instinct, your gut feeling or power of intuition, and choose the direction that speaks to you.

Being linked to lust and physical desire, the happy, pleasure seeking Woman rune may be encouraging you to connect with your sexual side. Indulge in carnal pleasures, enjoying the intimacy and sensuality that is experienced when you do. If such notions make you feel uncomfortable, Woman would invite you to explore your inner world and discover what pleases you. However, do not limit your understanding of pleasure to sex; the world is full of sensory experiences that thrill the senses. Discover all of these things as you ground yourself in the material world, enjoying the way that your body allows you to interact with the world around you.

The woman rune can point to the areas of your life in which you or somebody else is in need of healing. There is a nurturing aspect to this rune that counsels you to be gentle with yourself. Perhaps some time out is needed as you step away from a hectic schedule to find some time for yourself. Use this time to get to know yourself, understanding your emotional needs and desires. There is sometimes a people pleasing aspect to the Woman rune that means the desires of the self can go unfulfilled. Offer yourself the same compassion that you would share with others.

When Negative:
Woman can be indicating areas of your life where you are experiencing exhaustion and burn out. Examine the factors which are draining your cup and find a way to take a step back. Woman may also indicate an overbearing desire to micro-manage or interfere in a way that stifles the other. Resist the urge to control, allowing people space to learn in their own way as there is a delicate balance between nurturing and suffocating. Be mindful too, that not all people require the same type of care. As individuals,our personal needs can be wildly different, so adapt the care you give to suit what it is that you are caring for. After all, the water that nourishes the spider plant would drown the cactus.

As Woman recommends stillness, it might suggest that you are resisting this, being determined to move forward with something even though the timing is not ideal. If you are feeling impatient, examine why that is. Where does the need to rush derive from? It might suit you better to take your time so that important details are not overlooked.

When Woman appears in a reading it could suggest that the querent has a lack of receptivity to new ideas, coupled with a tendency to be dismissive. They may be displaying a stubborn streak, closing themselves off to the input from others. If this is the case, probe deeper into why this person is so fixated on a set idea that they find themselves unable to open their mind to new concepts.

If Woman resembles that which we receive, then it follows it may also symbolise the things that we reject. Perhaps something will be offered to you, in which case the appearance of this rune might be advising you to think very carefully about whether or not you wish to accept it. Be diligent as you make decisions, making sure that things are legitimate and above board. You do not have to say yes to every opportunity that presents itself. This rune can indicate a feeling of disconnection from your intuition and an inability to trust your own judgement. This is not something that can be solved in an instant, but you are being encouraged to tune into your inner knowing so that you may learn to listen to the subtle signals that your body gives you.

Questions to ask when Woman appears in a reading:
What do I wish to nurture?
What areas of my life might benefit from patience?
Do I make space for beauty, pleasure and comfort in my life?
What aspects of myself need healing?
How often do I spend introspectively examining my own thoughts?
Do I resist sitting in stillness?
Do I trust my intuition?
Do I allow others the space that they need?
Do I feel ready to receive?

Man

Keywords:

Action, decisive, direct, passionate, assertive, fiery, hasty, volatile, war, aggressive, powerful, courageous, reckless, defensive, combative, brave, honourable.

Associations:

Element: Fire/Air

Astrology: Aries

Deities: Ares/Mars

Spirit Archetypes: God, Warrior, Hero, Father Figure, Protector of the Innocent

Planet: Mars

Tarot Card: Emperor, Ace of Wands, Ace of Swords

The Man rune represents the masculine principle in a conceptual sense. As an expression of energy, it embodies the polar opposite of the Woman rune. If Woman represents Yin, then Man represents Yang and all that this symbolically represents in terms of direct action, assertiveness and forward momentum. Where Woman represents the earthly and watery elements, Man represents the elements of fire and air. The simple line drawing of an arrow could be likened to the instruments of direction that we see in the tarot- the sword and the wand. Both of these tools point and direct, taking aim with power and assertiveness at the intended direction. Figuratively, the wand projects our desires outward with intensity and passion, just as the sword cuts away unneeded matter to leave only what is strictly necessary. There is a pragmatic edge to the cold, hard steel of the sword that seeks precision and facts. The Man rune embodies confidence and courage, the fearlessness to chase after what you most desire. Man does not wait around patiently; the hasty, decisive nature of Man means that the individual takes immediate action to achieve their goals.

The Man rune can represent a father figure or protective guardian who boldly and courageously protects what they value. We could view Man as the embodiment of the humble warrior that valiantly protects those that they hold dear, or the natural leader who provides protection and safety for the community. Man speaks to our survival instincts, those innate forces that compel us to act as we do. Whilst we may learn to behave in a civilised fashion as society dictates, those raw, primal driving forces never really leave us. They lie dormant, until we encounter a situation that calls for survival. A delicate balance is needed so that we may walk the line between controlling our primal instincts and repressing them completely. These urges exist to protect us, but if we indulge them too much then we may cross the line into harming others with our behaviour.

Being ruled by the planet of Mars (the Roman equivalent of Ares), this rune carries the energy that we might associate with the Greek God of war and courage, Ares. Ares is a complex figure in Greek mythology. His warlike persona dominates his portrayal in Greek myth, but as he evolves within the Roman pantheon we see additional depth to his character that highlights his strength, bravery, and virility.

What it means in a reading:
When Man shows up in a reading it can be encouraging us to take the initiative and act in a direct way. If an opportunity presents itself, be swift and assertive, not delaying any more than is strictly necessary. It indicates that you are highly driven towards succeeding, and the early bird catches the worm in this situation, so be prepared to show up. The arrow of the Man rune can quite literally be pointing you in the direction of where you need to shift your focus and attention.

If you are involved in an uncomfortable situation, the Man rune may be here to advise you that honest, direct communication is the key. The time for sugar coating your words with subtlety has passed, now is the time to speak openly and truthfully. Do not be cruel, but express yourself authentically even if this means attracting the disapproval of others. Unpleasant situations will pass, but the liberty you gain by standing by your beliefs is crucial to your sense of well-being. Man is less concerned about gaining approval from others and more interested in doing what they wish to do.

The Man rune can represent powerfully motivating factors. It points us in the direction of our passion, driving us forward with a burning desire to achieve our aim. It can signify a busy period of heightened activity that calls for commitment and determination to see it through. Trust that what you are working towards will be worth it, and do not rest on your laurels by taking things for granted. The energy that you invest now is laying the foundation for what is to come. Let your decisions be dictated by what is rational and factual as you maintain a fair-minded sense of assertiveness. Ultimately, Man seeks to bring structure and stability into the world so that life will be orderly and equal. We are reminded though, that to see success we have to put the work in, even when it is challenging. Perseverance, tenacity and endurance are the strengths we need to bring about the change that we wish to see. Look to the surrounding runes for an indication of what motivates you.

Man may show up to encourage you to bravely stand up for yourself. If there is a tendency to shy away from conflict, explore why that is. If avoidance of confrontation is due to fear or lack of confidence then you may be encouraged to build your confidence so that others do not take advantage of you. It is up to you to be your own champion, defending yourself so that others do not take without limit. On the other hand, if you have the opportunity to defend a vulnerable person then do so. Society prospers when we all prosper so take care of those that need it, speaking out against injustice.

When Negative:
The negative aspects of Man can manifest as an abuse of physical power, blood lust and bullying. It can represent a person who enjoys conflict and stirs up unnecessary controversy to get a reaction from others. When out of balance, the assertive nature of Man is used not to maintain order, but rather to dominate and oppress for personal gain. Conversely, the negative manifestation of Man abandons all sense of order, becoming scattered and random.

When Man appears in a reading it may be a caution against reckless behaviour. There is an impulsive desire to react to a situation, but it would be wise to cool off a little before making any hasty decisions that you will later regret. It might be a primal instinct to take a heavy handed approach, but this may come off as brutish and aggressive. Give thought to the situation so that you combine the power of the intellect with that fiery passion. On the other hand, this rune can suggest that you are not taking enough practical steps to achieve your aim. Is there more that you could be doing to propel yourself forward?

Man indicates a person who holds power and influence; when such an individual has a moral compass that drives them to do what is best they can be a force for good, but the polarity of this would suggest a person who uses their power for their own gain with a desire to dominate others. If you are in a position of authority, be mindful of abusing power by bullying people or being too fierce. It is all too easy to slip into the role of tyranny if you let power go to your head.

Man can be headstrong; such a trait can be admirable, but the flexibility to change one's mind is important too. There could be a proclivity to jump to conclusions or over-react, such is the impulsive nature of this rune, but being quick to temper will not benefit you in the long run. If you know that you have a short fuse, become aware of the warning signs so that you can prepare yourself by taking steps to remove yourself from a volatile situation. Perhaps you simply need to step into another room and take some deep, calming breaths before you're ready to address the situation with a clear mind.

Expect the unexpected! The direct, fast acting essence of Man could materialise as something unexpected and sudden, an event that shakes up the status quo by derailing any plans you might have. When such events occur, even when they are disappointing, treat them as a learning experience. Such disruptions may be unwelcome but conflict can provide opportunities for growth and development.

Questions to ask when Man appears in a reading:
Am I as proactive as I could be?
Which areas of my life could benefit from an injection of motivation?
What am I intensely passionate about?
Do I stand up for myself and others?
Am I able to defend my beliefs and speak truthfully?
Can I be assertive when the situation calls for it?
How quick am I to make assumptions or jump to conclusions?
Do I have a tendency to behave recklessly?

Harvest

Keywords:
Abundance, fertility, order, planning, maturity, transformation, devotion, seasons, material goods, nourishment, growth, duty, responsibility, service to others.

Associations:
Element: Earth
Astrology: Virgo
Deities: Demeter/Ceres, Kore/Persephone
Spirit Archetypes: Mother Nature, Fertility Goddess, Maiden, Mother, Crone, Healer.
Planet: Mercury
Tarot Card: Temperance, Queen of Pentacles, Queen of Swords

The Harvest rune represents the success we experience when we place our time into nurturing something in a systematic, consistent way. It is the rune of plenty, but it differs somewhat from previous interpretations of this rune in that it has been attributed with the symbolism of Mercury rather than Jupiter. Mercury rules both Gemini and Virgo, so where the Flight rune takes on the Gemini aspects of Mercury, the Harvest rune embodies the Virgo aspect. Jupiter can indeed be seen to represent success and abundance, but it is the 'Mother Nature' aspect of Virgo that thematically corresponds closely with the Harvest.

It is straightforward to entwine the mythos of the Greek Goddess of Agriculture, Demeter with the symbolism of the Harvest rune. The harvest and agriculture are a logical pairing within the Witches' runes as the act of harvesting would surely fall under the domain of the Goddess of Grain who gifted humanity with knowledge of how to cultivate the land. Although Demeter, or Ceres to the Romans, is often associated with the zodiac sign of Virgo, there was a period when this constellation belonged to Astraea, the Goddess of Justice. She ruled for a time, but withdrew in disgust at the depravity of mankind. Today, Demeter, or her daughter Persephone, the

Goddess of Spring and Queen of the Underworld interlace with the symbolism of Virgo. This is a rational connection as the astrological Virgo season occurs during the harvest seasons in the northern hemisphere. As a 'Mother Nature' archetype, Demeter blessed humanity with an abundant harvest, but withdrew her bounty in despair when her daughter was taken to the Underworld by Hades. During her long, arduous search for her missing daughter, the earth withered and mortals starved. Persephone was eventually returned on Zeus' orders, but having eaten the fruit of Hades' realm she was bound to return for a portion of the year. This established a new order of the seasons; rather than flourishing all year, crops would only grow when Persephone returned from her Underworld interlude.

The story of these agricultural Goddesses lends this rune the symbolism of order, maturity and transformation as well as the obvious association of growth and abundance. It is Kore the maiden who descends into the Underworld, but it is Persephone the Queen who returns. Just as a seed germinates in the soil, so then, does the divine child transition into adulthood. As the survival of humanity is dependent on the crops, this means that the return of Persephone is imperative to maintain the cycle of life. It speaks of service to others, doing what needs to be done because our field of vision is wide enough to consider the bigger picture. It may seem unusual that Mercury rules Virgo when we think of the cunning, logical and knowledge seeking symbolism of this planet, but consider how cultivation of crops requires precision, planning and cooperation. The mercurial aspect of Virgo then, manifests as the systematic observation of the cycles coupled with meticulous attention to detail. A successful harvest requires precise knowledge of the land, climate and seeds, but it also needs consistent nourishment if it is to flourish. The intellect of airy Mercury combines with the fertile earthly aspects of Virgo to create an Earth Mother figure who is rational and regenerative. This makes this rune distinct form the Empress energy of the Woman rune which fixates on personal pleasure and sensory experiences.

What it can mean in a reading:
At face value, Harvest implies blessing, bounties and abundance. The fruits of your labour are about to pay off and you will reap the benefit of your effort. Harvest is closely connected to seasons and time, so this rune may be asking you to take stock of the timing or phase that you are in so you can get the most out of the situation. Is it time for planning, action or completion? Perhaps you need to finish up with your current projects before starting anything new, tying up the loose ends. In this way, Harvest can represent the endings that we welcome into our life, rather than ones we fear.

To harvest is to gather up or collect, but the groundwork for the harvest is prepared months in advance. In this sense, the Harvest rune may be reminding us to have a clear plan of action that paves the way for our long term goals. To achieve a goal, we must understand what is required, showing patience and devotion along the way. Don't expect immediate results, but show up consistently and you will see growth. Sacrifices may need to be made in the present in order to have a fulfilling future. Be shrewd in your choices so that you can take a calculated approach to how you invest your energy. Be mindful of the expression 'energy flows where attention goes'. The project before you may dominate your focus for the year ahead, so be sure that you are passionate enough about it before committing yourself to something that you may lose interest in.

There is an alchemy to the Harvest rune, a transformation that takes place in the womb of the earth. Due to the earthly nature of Harvest we often view this as the physical manifestation of our efforts that yield rewards in the form of money, a tangible unit of measurement. Let us consider though that this transformation may be of the self. It symbolises maturity, growing up or stepping into one's full potential. The Harvest rune may appear to affirm that you are fully equipped to move forward, encouraging you to be confident of your own abilities. It is easy for us to underestimate how far we have come, so this rune would affirm your skills.

Harvest may be asking you to consider what you can do for others; what gifts do you have to share that will enrich the lives of your fellow man? Be generous with your time, nurturing other people for the betterment of humanity. Spread joy where you can, as if scattering seeds upon the soil. Give thought too, as to what duties you have to uphold. It is easy to be disconnected from the very real harvests that take place every year, but the growing of food is one of the single most important jobs. Without it, there would be no fuel to nourish our bodies. In this sense, Harvest speaks to great responsibility, asking us to consider what our most important role is, taking stock of whether we are performing it to the best of our abilities.

When Negative:
On the negative side, Harvest can point to us being stuck in a certain phase of arrested development. Perhaps we are fixated on the 'idea gathering' aspect of a project and have no inclination to push through to the next step of putting those ideas in action. In addition to the practical aspects of life, this could also point to our personal development, causing us to examine if we are growing or remaining at a spiritual standstill. Harvest would remind us then, not to be overly rigid in our way of thinking. Whilst there is a process to follow, let go of the belief that the process is the ultimate authority. Knowledge evolves, so be prepared to evolve with it.

As a counterpart to the blooming fertility that Harvest may promise, it could also point to a deficit. The plans we laid out are not growing in the direction that we hoped. This is disappointing, but be mindful there are no mistakes, only lessons to be learned. Take comfort from these adverse situations by relishing the wisdom you have gained. The seasonal nature of Harvest also means that there will be future opportunities for your goals to flourish.

Harvest could also represent misdirected or scattered efforts. Do you have any type of plan in place, or are you taking an improvised, ad hoc approach? There are times to be creative and express yourself organically, but there are times when we must follow the established methods that have been studied and tested. You don't always need to reinvent the wheel; if there is a body of knowledge that has been curated over the centuries by experts who have devoted their life to research, begin by tapping into the existing knowledge base. Then you can approach your situation with insight into how things work, allowing you to invest your time into building upon what already exists.

Questions to ask when Harvest appears in a reading:
Where am I placing my attention?
Is there an existing body of knowledge that could help me achieve my goals?
Do I take a systematic approach to my projects?
Can I unify logic and compassion in order to have a balanced insight?
What am I willing to sacrifice to achieve my dreams?
Do I consistently show up?
Which areas of my life do I show maturity?
Are there any parts of my life where I feel stuck?
What do I do for others?
Do I work well as part of a team?

Crossroads

Keywords:

Choices, fate, destiny, decisions, stalemate, conflict, contests, options, sacrifice, bargaining, liminal, meeting, danger, adventure.

Associations:

Element: Fire

Astrology: Sagittarius

Deity: Hekate, Hermes, The Fates

Spiritual Archetypes: The Guide, Psychopomp, The Devil, Trickster, Chiron

Planet: Jupiter

Tarot Card: The Lovers, Judgement

The Crossroads depicts two double headed arrows crossing each other. At first we may view this as a crossroads in our life's journey, the point at which we are called to make a definitive decision about which path we will take. The sign at the crossroads points to multiple pathways, each promising a different destiny, but we can choose only one at a time. How will we know which is the right path to take, or if there even is a right path at all? This is a rune of dilemma and destiny, in which the path we choose will have far reaching implications that we cannot yet know. When faced with such choices we are compelled to turn inwards, evaluating our values and desires so we can be clear about what it is we hope to gain, making a deliberate, conscious choice. Whilst the majority of crossroads we encounter will be figurative in nature, the theme of the Crossroads also holds the essence of magic and liminality. Hekate was said to inhabit the Crossroads, earning her the name Trioditis, meaning 'Of the Three Roads'. It is a threshold, or a meeting point for different energies to converge. How many people have stood before a fork in the road as they made a decision that would impact their future? Every soul that passes through leaves a little energetic imprint on the Crossroads that imbues it with an ephemeral layer of magickal potential, marking it as a place for transition. Here is where we leave the old behind to step into the new as Hekate ushers us across the boundary of the old ways towards our destiny. Folk tales tell of people meeting mysterious entities down at the Crossroads who offer greatness that often comes with a hidden cost. One such myth has built up around Robert Johnson, a dedicated and exceptionally talented blues musician born in the early 20th century. Blues music and the Devil character are inextricably linked, and Johnson lent into this with the lyrics he wrote for his songs. Decades after his death, historians pieced together the legend of a twenty year old Johnson making a pact with the Devil at the Crossroads; whilst Johnson's skills as a musician are most likely down to devotion to his craft, the story has turned him into a legendary figure with an enduring legacy. The concept of bargaining away one's soul at the Crossroads could be seen to represent sacrifice; the path that leads to personal growth might require us to give something up before we can walk it. The Crossroads demands an offering before you can progress, but rather than your soul, it might be relationships or a sense of security that you need to leave behind. For this reason, Crossroads carries a sense of independence and adventure as the path that truly calls to you may require you to strip away your comforts. Dominion over the Crossroads has been transferred to Sagittarius, the independent, adventure seeking Centaur who relishes exploration and travelling down unknown paths. The brave archer continuously seeks self-improvement, which means never shying away from the potential dangers held on the road less travelled.

Viewed from a different perspective however, these arrows are no longer the boards of a wooden sign post, but weapons locked in battle. Two adversaries rooted in a deadly fight, neither able to best the other, their weapons crossed in a mutual stalemate. Such imagery speaks to conflict and obstacles not easily passed, representing struggle and difficult encounters. Rather than a plethora of options, we see that the way is blocked, the road ahead is closed off. We could interpret the cross of the Crossroads as a literal barrier, the 'X' that warns us of impending danger that lies ahead, or of the cautionary label we see on hazardous substances. When viewed as an X, Crossroads can also suggest errors or mistakes.

What it can mean in a reading:
When Crossroads shows up in a reading you may have reached a point where you can no longer juggle conflicting energy, you must choose a path to carry on with. You could be faced with an ultimatum which forces you to make a difficult decision. Choosing one thing will be at the expense of something else as having both isn't a likely option in this scenario. Contemplate what it is that you truly desire the most, carefully weighing up the situation so that you can make the decision that is best for you in this pivotal life moment. Conversely, the Crossroads may be a reassurance that your destiny is not something you can evade. Take comfort in knowing any choice you make is right for you because you can only ever be where you are supposed to be. Perhaps you are experiencing a period of adversity or chaos that makes you feel as if

your life is off track, when really there is no 'track'. Those times of struggle and uncertainty are inevitable for everyone at one stage or another, and unpleasant as they are, they shape us into the best version of ourselves if we open ourselves up to the lesson they provide. Perhaps, there are no wrong choices, only different choices.

Crossroads can indicate a moral dilemma where external influences challenge your core values and principles. Nobody can make a decision for you however, it is up to you to decide if your morals are worth compromising. Crossroads can only remind you that you should make your choice from a place of deepest authenticity and be prepared to stand by your decision even if the outcome is unfavourable. The act of bargaining is also implied by the Crossroads; perhaps you don't feel drawn to any of the options that are available to you, so why not invent your own way! Paths do not appear, they are created when you choose to walk them, therefore, lay out the terms of what you desire so that a mutually beneficial arrangement can be forged.

The appearance of Crossroads can indicate a meeting between yourself and somebody that offers you an attractive opportunity in the form of connections or skills that will enable you to step closer to your goals. It is possible that this relationship will have a 'mentor and apprentice' dynamic as they pass along their knowledge. Do be wary about anyone who offers something that is 'too good to be true' or asks for too much in exchange.

When Negative:
Crossroads can indicate difficulty in making a decision, perhaps being so afraid of making the 'wrong' choice that you feel unqualified to make any decision at all. However, be mindful that refusal to make a choice is in itself a choice as it holds just as much consequence as any deliberate selection. If fear mingles with anxiety to paralyse your decision making abilities then deep introspection is required to understand why. Do you trust your own judgement? What are you most afraid of? Crucial moments of choice usually carry with them a level of discomfort, but this is the price for transitioning to a more fulfilling set of circumstances. Do not put off your decision making for any longer than is strictly necessary.

At its most negative, Crossroads can indicate a feeling of being trapped, of having no choices available to you. This can leave you feeling helpless, as if every road leads to a dead end. As frustrating as this is, perhaps the path you are attempting to travel is simply not meant for you. It could be that you are not yet prepared for what this path would entail; examine what drives you in this direction, taking stock of what you could be doing to unblock the path. Are you as prepared as you think? Maybe you are being encouraged to delve deeper, consulting trusted sources and studying so that you are armed with the knowledge you need to adequately face the potential dangers.

The Crossroads rune might be warning you of a potential stalemate situation. Both yourself and your opponent possess equal amounts of skill and stubbornness that suggest an impasse. Ego might drive you to maintain a stoic position, but no progress will be made until somebody backs down. If you have examined your predicament from every angle and no compromise can be reached, then it might be time to consider stepping back. Crossroads may even be asking you to consider if your perspective in such a stalemate is accurate. Is it possible that you could be misinformed? Know that there is no shame in walking away from a deadlock situation or admitting that you are wrong as it takes courage to do both.

Questions to ask when Crossroads appears in a reading:
How confident am I in my ability to make decisions?
Do I feel able to accept the consequences of my choices?
How does it feel to consider that I might be incorrect in my assumptions?
Do I find it easy to make decisions?
What would I be willing to sacrifice in order to progress?
What are the potential consequences that I fear?
What crossroads am I facing right now?

Waves

Keywords:

Action, movement, purity, renewal, volatility, fluid, fickle, unpredictable, flux, mysterious, hidden depths, revelations, ripple effect, emotions, alluring.

Associations:

Element: Water
Astrology: Pisces
Deities: Poseidon/Neptune, Amphitrite
Spirit Archetypes: Undine, Sirens,
Mermaids, Leviathan
Planet: Neptune
Tarot Card: The Moon, Ace of Cups

The rune of the ocean waves offers up a stark sense of polarity. Waves are the ebb and flow of water that is emblematic of emotion. High tides are the peaks of intensity and euphoria, whilst low tides are the moments of gentle stillness and peace. The ocean can devour, and the ocean can give life. We see water as a symbol of renewal and purity as it dissolves away the residue of dirt that clings to an object. The cold splash of water against skin is rejuvenating, but we must always hold a healthy respect for the sea because gentle waves can so easily give way to a volatile current that rips us out of our depth. It would seem only logical to dedicate this oceanic rune to the planet Neptune, named for the Roman God of the Ocean, derived from the Greek God Poseidon.

When in a benevolent mood, Poseidon granted smooth seas to sailors and created new islands. However, when angered he struck his trident on the ground in temper, sending earthquakes, floods and springs. He could even withhold water to cause droughts. Poseidon represents the primordial waters that can be both placid and destructive. There is a duality to his power that exists within most archetypes; gentle flowing water is nourishing and replenishing to the land, but floods can be catastrophic. In this sense, Poseidon can offer abundance or deficiency, his temperament is as unpredictable as the great waters over which he governs.

The mythology surrounding Poseidon is far more erratic than the gentle, dreamy nature of Pisces which is the corresponding zodiac sign of this rune. Ethereal Pisces possesses a sensitive, deeply intuitive quality which once again serves to demonstrate the dual nature of the watery elements. When this rune appears in a reading, it will be up to the intuition of the reader to infer what type of message these waves are carrying. Where Poseidon represents the volatile side of water, Pisces represents the subtle intuitive and emotional side.

What it can mean in a reading:

Perhaps the first thing your eye notices about this rune is the fluid swirl of the waves, symbolic of the tidal motion of the sea. To interpret it then at face value we could read this as an advisory that our situation is in flux. Everything is liable to shift direction and change at a moment's notice, so we must be able to lean into the chaos of the situation and be prepared for the unexpected. There is an element of adventure though to this swirling disorder which can indicate a period of excitement.

Waves also offer us reassurance in times of deficiency that abundance will eventually return. The tide will turn, and what you are missing right now will eventually come back to you. The flip side to this notion would then warn us not to take for granted that what we are receiving now will remain constant. Be fluid, and ride the wave of life, liberated in the knowledge that nothing is forever.

Deep waters conceal an entire realm of mystery; the world beneath the surface is like another planet. Access to the bottom of the ocean is limited to humans, only with expensive apparatus can we descend to the ocean floor, but this too carries danger. Perhaps Waves has appeared in your casting to encourage you to find depth in the situation. Look inwards to discover how you really feel. Tuning in to your inner well of feeling can be difficult, but switch off your distractions and mediate so you may glimpse what lies deep within your psyche. Not only is this a well of emotions, but it is one of creativity too. Treasure will be found when you explore the ocean within you.

Continuing on the theme of emotion, this rune may suggest periods of heightened emotion, or an imbalance with our emotional state. Never one to bottle up his feelings, when Poseidon feels slighted he expresses his emotions of rage by summoning storms and sending great tremors through the earth. Let us consider then, that Waves may be encouraging you to release your emotions rather than bottling them up. Perhaps you have anger that needs an outlet, in which case, find a healthy way to release that emotion in a cathartic manner. Conversely, you might benefit from a good cry, primal scream into a pillow, or even a laughter session.

The fresh, purifying nature of water may suggest that you are entering a period of renewal. You may finally feel that you have washed away the emotional baggage and spiritual miasma of a past situation. Having healed from the hurts of previous experience, you are now ready to enter a new era of your life. As well as healing, Waves also speaks of the dissolution of boundaries. The sea has no concern for borders or earthly structures, eroding towns just as easily as coastal edges. Waves may be encouraging you not to be deterred by obstacles. Sometimes we encounter petty bureaucracy or gatekeeping, but this rune advises you to flow right past them. Water always finds a way; if there is no path then it creates one. Honour the boundaries that protect you, but diffuse the ones that would otherwise hold you stagnant.

When negative:

Waves can speak to the element of temptation that water beguiles us with. The open waters are expansive, promising adventure and excitement. The downside to this however is one of danger. Perhaps there is a level of risk involved by venturing into unknown territories. This connection between allurement and danger is embodied in the archetype of the mermaid. Beautiful women from the waist up and fish from the waist down, mermaids have a reputation for luring in sailors then drowning them in the deep. These mysterious beings seem so gentle and ethereal but they can conceal nefarious intent. In a reading then, perhaps Waves warns us of illusion and temptation as a means to help us avoid danger.

As the tide recedes in its daily rhythm, the shoreline reveals more than it does at high tide. This maximum exposure means that there is more to be seen as the sea reveals its secrets. Be mindful then, that this rune can indicate something is about to be revealed. The tide will roll back on what was previously hidden, possibly bringing information to light that you don't feel ready to share.

A fickle nature is suggested by the Waves rune; try not to rely too heavily on a person as there is a chance that they might change their mind suddenly, essentially pulling the rug from beneath you. This can leave you floundering, so be sure that you have back up plans and alternative options. It might be that the person or organisation you are dealing with is particularly erratic and there is too much uncertainty surrounding them for you to put your trust in them. Like the sea, some people have a wayward, whimsical way about them. They can't be contained or tied down, and as much as we may want to find stability with them, it's their capricious nature that draws us to them. In such cases, we simply have to admire such people from afar for fear of being dragged down to the depths.

Waves can indicate that you are feeling overwhelmed. Whatever set of circumstances you are dealing with, it's too much. As soon as you handle one obstacle, another wave crashes down. It is unlikely to stay this volatile forever, so you may need to put your plans on hold or take a step back as you wait for a better opportunity to progress.

Questions to ask when Waves appears in a reading:
What, if anything, are you suppressing in your inner depths?
Do you have a tendency to stick to surface level exploration only?
What outlets do you have for emotional expression?
How capable are you at adapting to highly changeable situations?
What tempts you right now?
Are you in touch with your emotions?
Do you feel able to express your emotions to others?

Star

Keywords: Hope, success, guidance, wishes, dreams come true, ideals, freedom, equality, enlightenment, visionary, virtue, gifts, honesty, trustworthy

Associations:

Element: Air

Astrology: Aquarius

Deities: Prometheus

Spirit Archetypes: Rebel, Free-thinker, Guide or Guardian, Fairy Godmother, Champion of Virtue, Celebrity.

Planet: Uranus

Tarot Card: The Star

The Star is an effervescent symbol of magic, happiness and success. It is the rune of wishes coming true, of achieving your ultimate desire. Glimmering in a sea of darkness, stars are only visible in the inky black of night but they are always there to offer a beacon of hope. Stars form constellations that act as a compass across the ether, they help us to orient ourselves and find our way, making them emblematic of the guidance we need when we are lost. To become a star is to be top of your field, celebrated for outstanding skill or achievement that elevates you to a position of high regard.

The Star rune is associated with the astrological sign of Aquarius, portrayed by the Cup-bearer, Ganymede. Ganymede was a handsome young man, taken by Zeus to Olympus to hold the coveted position of Cup-bearer and gifted with eternal youth and immortality. The role of a Cup-bearer is to serve drinks to a person of high ranking, ensuring that the beverage is free from poison. This is a position of privilege as it shows a bond of immense trust and a level of intimacy that offers the Cup-bearer the opportunity to effect change by influencing the mind of the one they serve. The myth surrounding Aquarius and its ruling planet Uranus doesn't quite line up as neatly as it does with the other planets and runes. Venus, for example, has consistently embodied concepts of relationships, harmony and beauty. Presently, we speak of the 'Age of

Aquarius' as a period of transcendence, enlightenment and liberty, when the shackles of oppression are cast off for good. It is difficult to see how revolutionary thinking aligns with the mythos of the Cup-bearer, but if Aquarius is the visionary and free-thinker, perhaps then it is logical that it can't be easily labelled or pinned down. By this reasoning, the archetype of the Star might be better represented by Prometheus, the Titan who stole fire from the Gods and gifted it to the mortals. Prometheus went against the status quo, defying the Gods in an act of rebellion that transformed the existence of humanity. The gift of fire changed the world, offering heat, light and the ability for craftsmanship to flourish. Prometheus is the divine rebel, the outlier who revolutionised and liberated humanity with the luminous flames. If being exalted to the status of 'Star' means standing out and excelling in your field by going against the grain, then Prometheus, the friend of mankind, achieved this.

What it can mean in a reading:
The Star can represent your inner most desires and ambitions. It is the expression of your dreams and wishes, so consider the position of this rune in a reading. When it falls far away from the other runes it may act as a beacon of hope that although you have a long path ahead of you, you are on the right track. When it lands in a central position it could be a strong indication that the stars are aligning right now. Everything seems to be falling into place in a way that makes this the ideal moment to act.

As a symbol of virtue, the Star may be a reminder to stick to your principles. Doing what you believe to be right and acting from a place of authenticity will serve you best. If the Cup-bearer is a trusted individual then the Star might be your message to behave honourably, offering sincere loyalty to those around you. Alternatively, the Star could indicate a person in your life who is honest, trustworthy and filled with good intentions. Continuing on the theme of trust, the Star would remind us to trust the process. Sometimes a leap of faith is called for, taking a chance on the unknown in the hope that it works out well.

When you're feeling lost and unsure about the path you are walking, the Star is your affirmation that you are not as lost as you think. Just as the North Star offers guidance to travellers, know that there will be someone who will offer you similar guidance. Don't be afraid to reach out and ask for help when you have lost your bearings. Similarly, be a guide to others when you have the opportunity to do so, acting as a light in the dark to those who are unsure of the way.

If you want to experience success, then the Star might be here to encourage you to aim higher than you ever thought you could. It encourages you to believe in yourself and to believe that your dreams are achievable. Whether you believe you can, or you believe you can't, you are right. The first step to getting what you want is imagining that it is possible. Visualise it, experience how it would feel as you reframe your way of thinking to believe this could happen for you. When you operate from a foundation of firm self-belief, the way ahead will light up for you.

There is an aura of luck and destiny to the Star rune. Perhaps you are meant to achieve great things, and no matter how far you step away from the path, you always find yourself pulled back. Maybe you often experience serendipitous moments; seemingly wrong choices that lead to positive outcomes. Fortune smiles upon you when this rune appears, suggesting you will be blessed with advantages that help you propel.

There is an individualistic quality to the Star that carries the message to be yourself. There is no need to be like everyone else. People rarely achieve spectacular things by following the masses. Don't be afraid to be different, to stand out by thinking or acting in a way that is perceived as unusual by society; your unique qualities are your gifts, and these ought to be cherished. Perhaps you have the opportunity to shake things up a bit, opening people's eyes and their minds to an alternative way of thinking. This is the free-spirited, visionary aspect of the star that aims to do what has never been done before.

When negative:
Over idealistic ways of thinking could be suggested by the Star. Whilst optimism is beneficial, being too naive or idealistic leaves you open to intense disappointment, as well as increasing the likelihood of being taken advantage of. Assess your situation, asking for help from a trusted source if you don't feel that you can be objective in your viewpoint.

As a badge of honour, the Star would ask if you are behaving in an honourable and trustworthy way. Are you attempting to use trickery or unethical methods to achieve your goals? Give thought to the long term implications of using such tactics; will you be proud of using such means and could there be unwanted consequences? The Star may also be a warning that those around you are perhaps not as trustworthy as they appear.

The humanitarian aspect of the Star speaks of doing good things for humanity as a whole. In its negative manifestation then, this rune would ask us to examine our motives. Are they selfless or selfish? Be honest with yourself about what motivates you and assess whether such self-interest could ultimately do more harm than good. Give thought to what you have to offer others that would improve life for the majority.

When negative, the Star may indicate a loss of faith and a feeling of no direction. Perhaps you are experiencing a dark night of the soul and everything seems hopeless. A lack of faith coupled with a loss of hope can feel like a period of depression, but don't struggle alone. If you can truly see no way through your current situation then you must ask for help rather than suffering in silence. Once again you are asked to trust that there are people out there who care.

A lack of ambition may be signified when the Star is in an unfavourable position; it might be that you are drastically underestimating your talents and are not dreaming big enough. There should be no limit on how high you dream! If you set your goals too low then you deny yourself the opportunity to truly shine. Consider why this may be, are you afraid of shining too brightly?

Questions to ask when Star appears in a reading:
What is my deepest desire?
What am I aiming for?
Am I trustworthy and honest?
Do I believe that my dreams are achievable?
How often do I help other people?
Do I know where I am going in life?
What ideals do I hold?

Scythe

Keywords:

Endings, separation, maturity, wisdom, mastery, restriction, discipline, completion, sudden changes, finality, organisation, letting go, release

Associations:

Element: None

Astrology: Scorpio, Capricorn

Deities: Kronos/Saturn, Hades/Pluto

Spirit Archetypes: The Reaper, Tyrant, Dictator, Strict Mentor.

Planet: Pluto, Saturn

Tarot Card: Death, Tower, Wheel

The Scythe is a sickle shaped blade used to cut crops that are ready for harvesting. As a universal symbol of death, the Scythe can at first appear frightening; the talisman of the grim reaper, it severs consciousness just as it separates the wheat from the stalk. In this sense, it may signify endings, heartbreaks, and the pain that accompanies letting go. That being said, it is important not to fear this rune as endings are a natural and necessary component of existence. It ought to be stated that seeing the Scythe in a reading does not mean that you or the querent are about to die; it speaks to endings in a broader sense, being far more likely to indicate the end of a particular set of circumstances. Such scenarios are limitless, but could include feelings, ideas, relationships or trends. It is normal to feel sombre when something cherished comes to an end but this rune reminds us that we cannot hold onto things forever. Life is a cycle of beginnings and endings, and we must learn to savour each moment while we have it. When the time comes to let go, we must do so with grace and gratitude, acknowledging the pain, but also embracing the promise of new beginnings that lie ahead.

Remember that although the Scythe cuts away the grain, it does not do this to destroy the crop. Rather, it denotes the end of the yearly cycle, harvesting the fruits of the land and preparing the earth for future growth. As a tool, it is used for necessity not cruelty.

The agricultural symbolism of the Scythe shows us that time is cyclical and eternal, ebbing and flowing in a seasonal rhythm. The plant is sacrificed to provide the fuel that nourishes and ensures continued growth. Such an ending is integral because we cannot linger forever in an eternal summer.

The symbolism of the Scythe overlaps with the mythos of both Hades and his father Kronos. Hades is the Greek God of the Underworld who rules all that belongs under the earth. Described as 'inexorable', Hades had a reputation for being utterly steadfast and unmoveable in his duties that centre on maintaining order and justice. He is usually impartial and neutral, being less interested in torturing souls and more consumed with guarding the entrance to his home that protects the threshold between life and death. Once someone passes into the realm of Hades, they seldom return. Such is the finality of some endings. Kronos, on the other hand, plays the role of the castrator, severing the bond between his Mother Gaia and Father Ouranos, the Earth and the Sky. Myth tells how he used a sickle to cut off the genitals of Ouranos, casting the severed penis into the sea and destroying his father in the process. This earned Kronos the position of ruler and God of the Harvest, but he too became a tyrant that would also meet his end at the hands of his children. Kronos tried to evade his fate by devouring his offspring, but his attempts to alter his destiny were in vain, because some things are inevitable. The planet Saturn, with its restrictive rings, takes its name from the Roman interpretation of Kronos. The sphere of influence of Saturn included time and dissolution as well as the harvest.

What it can mean in a reading:
The Scythe indicates that it is time to let go. We must sever ties with things or people to whom we have a deep emotional bond, and whilst this act of letting go can be excruciatingly painful, it is a necessary part of our spiritual growth. By releasing what no longer serves us, we create space for new opportunities, experiences, and relationships to enter our lives. While these moments may leave us reeling in anguish, it's important to remember that such pain is often the echo of immense joy we once experienced. The things we cherish most are also the things that, at times, cause us the greatest heartache. This is the bittersweet beauty of life; mourn your losses, acknowledge your pain, but never lose sight of the potential for healing and renewal as it is important to find hope amidst sorrow. Whilst you are mourning the end of a phase in your life, know that you are paving the way for a new era to commence, which you shall enter with more wisdom, maturity and knowledge than you had before.

On a happier note, the Scythe may indicate that you have completed something deeply challenging, suggesting a welcome ending. Perhaps it was a feat of endurance that tested you at every turn. The obstacles and challenges experienced have no doubt bestowed you with skills and understanding that you would not have otherwise gained. Drawing upon the symbolism of the Scythe once more as an agricultural implement, agriculture is an incredibly important skill cultivated by humanity that raises our quality of life. Understanding the process of growing crops took our ancestors a long time to learn. If they had not invested their time into understanding the process, we would not experience the luxury of easy access to food that we have today. Trials and sacrifice were required to master the art of agriculture, serving as a reminder to sacrifice short term pleasure for long term gains.

Perhaps the Scythe is asking you to sacrifice something now in order to achieve your long term goals. The notion of sacrifice suggests a level of discomfort as you let go of certain pleasures that may be keeping you dormant. Perhaps you need to give up an indulgent habit or expensive membership for a short while if you are to save time and money. Like a ticking clock, the Scythe is a reminder that our time is a finite resource and it must be used wisely if we are to reap the benefits. Structure, routine and restraint help us to allocate our time responsibly.

When Negative:
On the negative side, the Scythe can suggest refusal to let go of something that is harmful to you in a physical, emotional or spiritual way. This could be clinging on to a relationship with someone who openly disrespects you, or lingering in a job when a string of false promises are made. The 'sunk cost fallacy' often causes us to commit to situations that are draining us of time and money because of how much we have previously invested. However, no amount of waiting will ever bring back what has been lost, so the Scythe counsels you to sever this connection. Walk away once and for all rather than squandering any more of your precious energy. It can also indicate a person who feels unable to venture outside of their comfort zone, even though they have outgrown it. When we do this, we stunt our own growth due to a fear of letting go.

The Scythe may also hold up a mirror to the ways in which we misspend our time and resources; perhaps there is a resistance to forming any kind of plan, coupled with a lack of comprehension about the time constraints that you have. Take stock of your resources and use them wisely. There is a cyclical element to the Scythe as new growth is promised, but embracing this energy requires us to be flexible. Rigidity and inflexibility can manifest as resistance to the inevitable seasonal cycles.

The sharp curved blade of the Scythe could indicate one is too quick to cast things aside, cutting off relationships and opportunities without ever giving them a chance to develop into something deeper. If this is the case, examine why there is a need to cut and run. Sometimes, people who are deeply afraid of being abandoned will separate from others prematurely so that they can avoid the pain of being the one who gets cast aside. In this sense, the Scythe may represent a person who comes across as cold and unyielding, never opening up or forming attachments to anyone.

Sadness and grief are natural, human responses to experiencing loss. However, if despair descends into depression that you cannot see a way out of it is vital that you reach out for support. Do not suffer in silence.

Questions to ask when Scythe appears in a reading:
What do I need to cut out of my life?
Where do I resist endings and changes?
Am I comfortable acknowledging my emotions when I experience loss?
Do I use my time productively?
What am I holding on to that I should let go of?
How easy do I find it to release what no longer serves me?

Eye

Keywords:
Initiation, clarity, understanding, knowledge gained, mysteries revealed, intuition, protection, what is visible, attention.

Associations:
Element: Spirit/Ether
Astrology: None/Yours
Deities: All
Spirit Archetypes: The self, The Mystic, Witch, Seer, Protector
Planet: None, The Cosmos
Tarot Card: High Priestess

The Eye represents vision in both a physical and metaphysical sense. It is the sudden clarity that allows us to see the truth of the matter as well as the lifting of the ephemeral veil that grants us access to our intuition to see beyond the mundane. The eye reveals life's mysteries; initiating us into expanded consciousness, fresh knowledge and deeper wisdom. That which once deceived us no longer holds influence as the Eye bestows us with truth and understanding. Look to the runes close by to understand what you need to see.

This rune can represent the physical eye as well as the third eye, the conceptual eye which has the ability to see the unseen. When we speak of using our third eye, it refers to using our intuition or second sight in order to perceive the barely perceptible signals that our environment sends us. A noise so distant as to be virtually inaudible, or a micro-expression that lasts less than a second on the face of someone who is trying to deceive you. These are the things that we do not see, yet they raise an alarm within us. These signals are below the threshold of perception for our normal senses, but our third eye sees them. It raises the hairs on our arms and makes our stomachs flutter; we must heed these warnings as they are there to protect us.

Symbolically, the Eye represents omnipotence, the all-seeing, all-knowing force that is all around, alluding to a higher power or universal consciousness. The Eye is the silent watcher who witnesses the past, present and future without judging. The Eye has long been used as a symbol for wisdom and protection as the watchfulness of the Eye implies divine guidance; the watcher protects those that are watched. For this reason, it is not associated with a specific planet; instead we may choose to view the Eye as symbolic of the seat of consciousness, encompassing the universe.

The Eye is an enduring symbol through human history. Starting with ancient Egypt we see the Eye of Horus as a protective amulet, whilst the Eye of Providence, the Eye nestled inside a triangle, has been used since the 16th century as a Christian symbol, before being adopted by the Freemasons as a symbol of spiritual enlightenment. Five thousand year old figurines unearthed from modern day Syria can be counted amongst the oldest eye artefacts according to Potts (2021). So simple as to be devoid of almost all detail apart from two large eyes that dominate the face region. Known as the Tel Brak figures, we have no proof what these mysterious figurines represent, but some scholars have interpreted them as evidence of an 'Eye Goddess' cult of worship. In addition to representing the higher power of a divine figure, the Eye can also represent the self. You could view this literally when performing a reading, using the position of the Eye rune as a point of reference for the other runes, or perhaps you might view it as your higher self, pointing you towards the path you need for growth.

What it can mean in a reading:
When the Eye appears, it may indicate that although things appear straightforward, you are being encouraged to look beyond the surface, past what is obvious and down to the true nature. Things are not exactly as they seem, and you must tune into your intuition in order to navigate the situation safely. Everyone of us has the ability to tap into our mind's psychic abilities so if you feel disconnected from this side of yourself then perhaps now is the time to explore your gifts. Maybe you have premonitions that show up as visual images or sounds, or perhaps your dreams are a source of hidden information. Find a way to cultivate your abilities through consistent practice. In addition to encouraging us to develop our intuitive sight, the Eye may be encouraging us to look in a tangible, practical sense. Use your powers of observation to pay attention to what is happening around you. The human ability to see what we want to see, or expect to see, is remarkable. It allows us to go about our lives assuming that everything is exactly as it appears, but by shifting our conscious attention to the present, noticing behaviour, watching what others do, we may gain new insights into our circumstances. Look to the surrounding runes for an indication of what you see clearly, and what is obscured. Runes close to the eye indicate what is known, but runes that land in such a way as to be far away or obscured by other runes may be an indication of what is hidden from sight. As a rune of action, the Eye may convey the message that now is the time to observe rather than to act. Material knowledge, when

combined with spiritual knowing, provides a balanced perspective that helps you make choices from a place of wisdom.

The appearance of the Eye could indicate that a mystery will soon be revealed to you; you are ready to receive new knowledge and are about to become privy to new information that will be beneficial to you. However, as the Eye can also represent the self, it may suggest that you need to be introspective; develop self-awareness by looking inside yourself and examine your own thoughts through meditation or journaling. The answers that you are looking to find cannot be found from an outside source; tune out environmental distractions so that you may turn your eye inwards in a place of stillness. Reflect on your actions so that you become aware of the impact you have on those around you. Without expectation or judgement, simply observe what comes up for you as you make sense of what you are thinking and feeling.

If the eye signifies what we can see, then it could also indicate what can see us. Perhaps we are very visible at this moment in time, or are about to experience a moment in the spotlight where all attention is turned on us. This could be positive or negative depending on the situation. From a more comforting perspective, the Eye could indicate that somebody is watching over us, lending guidance and assistance from a distance. Depending on your beliefs, you may view this as a spirit guardian or a person here on the earthly plane.

When Negative:
As a negative manifestation of the Eye, it could suggest that somebody is watching you too closely. Could it be a colleague who wants to steal your ideas, or a person with an unhealthy interest in you? Perhaps you are being monitored by someone who wants to catch you stepping out of line. Keep your guard up and protect yourself from prying eyes at this moment. If you are aware of a specific person who behaves jealously towards you, avoid flaunting yourself or oversharing information so that you do not give them any extra ammunition that feeds their envious thoughts.

The Eye rune may advise that you are over exposed to something that is having a negative impact. Too much screen time, obsessive behaviour, or over indulgence in fantasy may be skewing your perspective. Examine what you are giving too much of your attention to so that you may apply moderation. Perhaps too much of your attention is projected into either the past or the future; in which case the Eye would remind you to observe this present moment, keeping your focus rooted in the now.

As a steadfast symbol of vision, it follows that the Eye could indicate our lack of vision or inability to see a person or situation for what it truly is. Perhaps we hold a distorted perspective that has been influenced by past experiences, or we are not seeing the bigger picture. Something may be preventing us from seeing ourselves or our environment clearly. On occasion, this rune might indicate that there are things being deliberately concealed from us. Look closely to uncover who or what is hiding something from you so that you may bring the truth to light.

This rune offers a caution against being too fixated on appearances. Cultivating beauty in your environment, or having a healthy amount of pride in appearances is beneficial to an extent, but do not allow it to prevent you from experiencing the world in a meaningful way. Things do not always have to look perfect in order to be special. In this way, the Eye counsels balance. It encourages us to observe the world through our physical vision and our inner vision, but both need to operate together. Relying on one at the expense of the other would cause an imbalance in our perspective.

Questions to ask when Eye appears in a reading:
What do I see clearly?
How can I see what is in my blind spot?
Do I really see myself clearly?
Are there factors that could be skewing my perception?
How do I want to be seen?
Do I bring my full attention to the present moment?
Am I protecting myself against unwanted attention?
How can I gain more insight into the matter at hand?

Sample Readings

Whilst learning a new skill, it can be beneficial to receive a visual reference that offers a practical example. This section will explore sample readings, offering a variety of interpretations for the readings. You can use this opportunity to practice your reading technique by drawing your own conclusion before you read the explanations given.

Reading One

Question: What steps should I take to improve my financial situation?

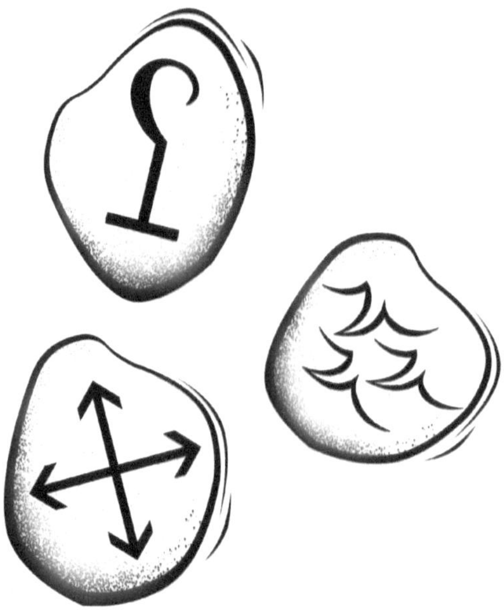

A small handful of stones was selected from the bag and cast in the free-form method. Three runes, Scythe, Flight and Crossroads landed face up in a triangle formation. The triangular formation suggests a harmony between the three runes, offering an answer that is a combination of all three energies. Reading them clockwise, starting with the Scythe, it is suggested that the querent needs to cut something loose and move away from a situation that is draining them. If they remain in their current circumstance they will not be able to progress. Flight suggests that swift movement is needed, whilst Crossroads implies that they need to choose an alternate path. Perhaps the querent has lingered too long in their comfort zone, or in an unhappy situation.

They probably know that it is time to move on, but fear of the unknown, of taking a risk, may be stopping them from reaching their potential. The fiery energy of Crossroads coupled with the airy energy of Flight imply that quick decisions and decisive action are needed. The querent needs to take a leap of faith and change the direction. Drastic change is needed for them to reach their full potential. Nobody is coming to offer them anything, they need to proactively pursue what they desire by separating themself from the methods that have not yielded success.

Alternate Interpretation:

The Crossroads, falling closest to the querent, is the dominant rune, therefore the theme of Crossroads dictates the theme of this reading, one of dilemmas and choices whereby the querent is standing at a literal or figurative fork in the road. The appearance of two additional runes represent the two choices on the table. Should they stay or go? Take the opportunity or not? The Crossroads is literally pointing to two divergent paths, suggesting that one path leads to the Scythe and the other leads to Flight. Scythe may represent a choice that calls for discipline and offers little flexibility, whilst Flight may indicate a path that is erratic and fickle, but offers more freedom. Scythe is associated with Pluto which is tied to wealth, but the wealth under the earth is by no means easy to achieve; you only make gains through toil and sweat but profit is highly likely if the querent is willing to dedicate themself to mastery. Flight, being ruled by Mercury, might seem like the more appealing option. Mercury is a silver tongued trickster who uses persuasive language to tempt, but there may be a hidden agenda. Quick wins are likely, but this path is unpredictable.

Reading Two

Question: How can I make more friends now I live in a new area away from everyone I know?

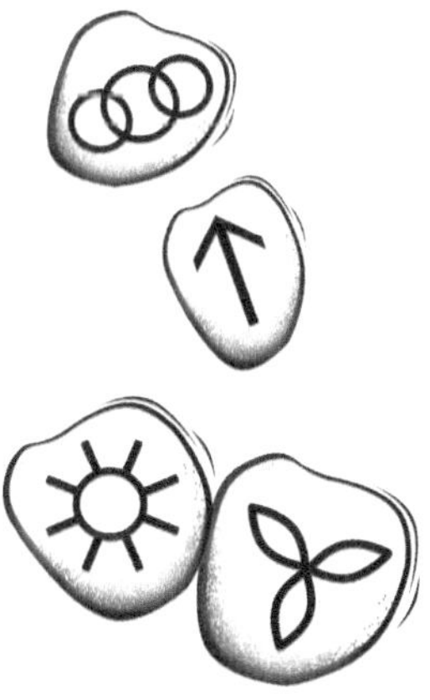

Another free-form cast was made, but this time four runes were pulled from the bag. Sun and Romance are touching, suggesting that these two stones support each other. Man has landed slightly above, and is pointing to the Rings. We might interpret from the flow of the reading that the querent needs to take on board the advice of Sun and Romance before they can move towards the community offered by Rings. The Sun represents the ego and self esteem, whilst Romance stands for love of the self, confidence and sharing. Perhaps the querent struggles with shyness and keeps them self closed off. This makes it even harder to form friendships as an adult. The querent could consider working on their relationship with the self, discovering what they like about themselves and celebrating their individuality.

They do not need to be or do anything other than they are, but they need to find a way to be comfortable with who they are. Romance indicates that being open and vulnerable with others could be a barrier. Being withdrawn may be interpreted as closed off or unfriendly. They may find it easier to form connections if they focus on asking genuine questions, then being prepared to answer the questions in return. The Sun suggests that they have a natural charisma, but are perhaps lacking belief that they have anything to share. Once they resolve this mental obstacle about fears of being unlikeable, they will naturally form friendships organically.

Alternate Interpretation:
Taking a planetary perspective on the reading, we can observe that there are runes of Venus (Romance) and Mars (Man), two planets that represent balancing, yet opposing forces. They are in a straight line with Rings, suggesting that when the querent's 'Mars' and 'Venus' energy is in alignment, they will make friends easily. However, the Sun rune is touching Romance, the rune of Venus, perhaps indicating that the querent needs to bring their Venus energy of the Romance rune to the surface. Currently, there is an imbalance. If the querent is too dominated by Man (Mars) then they might be coming across as overly forward, intense or intimidating to others. Sun is appearing to cast its bright beams on Romance, asking the querent to lean into their softer energy. Don't try to force or coerce, instead adopt a more free and easy attitude. You won't click with everyone you meet, but trust that those with whom you share a genuine connection will gravitate towards you. They need to give people space to come to them.

Reading Three

Question: Please tell me what I need to know at this moment in time.

The querent asked for a general reading, and four runes landed face up. The Star is
furthest away on its own, whilst the other three runes are clustered together in a
triangle. This suggests that the Star is the eventual outcome if the lesson of Waves,
Harvest and Flight is understood. The querent needs to give thought to their hopes and
aspirations if they are to ever come to light. Flight asks the querent to give thought to
what those hopes and dreams are? Are they aware, and do they dare to even dream or
set goals that they consider barely possible? Harvest speaks of a need to plant the seeds
of action, no matter how small. If the seeds of ideas are never planted then they can
never grow! The querent needs to form a plan, and Waves is a message to nurture those
plans with their attention and energy, but be mindful that it is natural for circumstances
to ebb and flow like the ocean tide. They should not lose hope just because they don't
see immediate results, it will take a long time for their actions to ripple outwards, but
trust that they will in time.

Alternate Interpretation:

The distance of the Star in this reading implies that the most cherished dreams and
aspirations seem hopelessly out of reach at the moment, but Harvest offers hope,
suggesting they may be closer than they realise. They still have put the work in, pouring
their effort and energy, but they are on the precipice of seeing their dreams bloom into
existence. They are reminded by Waves and Flight not to rest on their laurels though;
there is still work that needs to be done. They must continue to stay sharp and focused;
Flight advises them to keep the bigger picture in their mind by maintaining a 'birds eye
view' of the whole situation and not getting hyper-fixated on any one thing.

Reading Four

Question: What can I do to find peace when I feel so angry all the time?

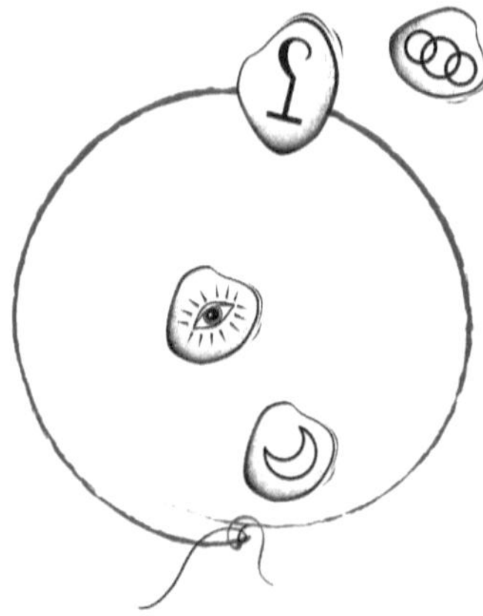

This reading was performed using the circle or loop method, whereby a length of string is fashioned into a circular shape on a flat surface. The centre of the circle is the heart of the matter, the top of the circle represents consciousness, the lower region represents subconsciousness and things outside of the circle represent external influences. The Eye rune represents the core message of the reading; it could be suggesting that the querent is disconnected from their spirituality. Perhaps they view spiritualism as something trivial or irrelevant, or they may approach spiritual growth from a shallow perspective, never diving deeper into what their core values are. The position of the Moon rune in the subconscious position suggests inner confusion. The disconnect between the conscious and subconscious mind runs deep, causing them to experience strong emotional reactions (such as anger) that they can't quite explain. Rings lies outside of the circle, indicating that the external factors that have caused this confusion could be coming from a community that the querent is part of. Could it be that an organisation or structure of some kind has imposed their views on them in a way that feels unnatural or unwanted? This could be an organized religion that they grew up into, or a group of friends with a narrow minded outlook. The position of the Scythe rune, straddling the perimeter of the circle, suggests that the querent needs to cut this group out of their life if they are to ever find peace. Only then can they begin to unravel the threads of suffering in their psyche and gain clear sight into what vexes them. In a way, the querent needs to discover who they truly are when they are out from the influence of this group. The judgment from others may have clouded their vision, and the anger that they experience is discontent caused by being out of alignment with their true self.

Alternate Interpretation:

The Eye represents everything that the querent can clearly see, with all that falls within the loop representing the field of vision. From this we can deduce that they are in touch with their emotions, perhaps a sensitive person who feels everything intensely. Being that they are tuned in to their emotional inner world, they struggle to understand why they find themselves feeling irritable and aggressive to those around them. This clouds their ability to find stillness, but it is the things outside of their field of vision that are causing the difficulty. Rings, being outside of the circle, could represent a person that the querent has a relationship with, who is the source of conflict. This could be a friend, family member or business partner. In this instance, the querent is oblivious to how damaging this relationship is, and the Scythe rune would encourage them to examine the behaviour of the people in their environment to identify who doesn't have their best interests at heart. They may not necessarily need to cut the person out, but they would need to confront them so that they could cut out the damaging behaviour.

Bibliography

Barnes, Michael P. *Runes: A Handbook*. Boydell Press, 2012

Corby, Dana. The Witches' Runes: A Traditional Divination System. United States: Independently Published, 2018.

Croce, Nicholas., Taft, Michael. *Greek Gods & Goddesses*. United States: Britannica Educational Publishing, 2013.

Fitch, Ed. Magical Rites From The Crystal Well (Llewellyn's Practical Magick). United States: Llewellyn Publications, 1984.

Guttman, Ariel., Guttman, Gail., Johnson, Kenneth. Mythic Astrology: Internalizing the Planetary Powers. United States: Llewellyn Publications, 1993.

Hudson, Benjamin. The Picts. Germany: Wiley, 2014.

Potts, Albert M.. The World's Eye. N.p.: University Press of Kentucky, 2021.

Rengel, Marian., Daly, Kathleen N. Greek and Roman Mythology, A to Z. United States: Facts On File, Incorporated, 2009.

Saille, Harmonia. *The Spiritual Runes: A Guide to the Ancestral Wisdom*. John Hunt Publishing Limited, 2009

Sheppard, Susan. A Witch's Runes: How to Make and Use Your Own Magick Stones. United States: Carol Publishing Group, 1998.

Wimmer, Gary L. *Lithomancy, The Psychic Art of Reading Stones*. Createspace Independent Publishing Platform, 2011